THE PLANT-BASED COOKBOOK

Inspiring | Educating | Creating | Entertaining

© 2020 Quarto Publishing Group USA Inc.

First published in 2020 by Chartwell Books,
an imprint of The Quarto Group
142 West 36th Street, 4th Floor
New York, NY 10018 USA
T (212) 779-4972 F (212) 779-6058
www.QuartoKnows.com

Chartwell titles are also available at discount for retail, wholesale, promotional, and bulk purchase. For details, contact the Special Sales Manager by email at specialsales@quarto.com or by mail at The Quarto Group, Attn: Special Sales Manager, 100 Cummings Center Suite 265D, Beverly, MA 01915 USA.

10 9 8 7 6 5 4 3 2 1

ISBN: 978-0-7858-3859-3

Library of Congress Cataloging-in-Publication Data

Names: Petitto, Melissa, author.
Title: The plant-based cookbook : 100 delicious recipes for a healthy life
/ Melissa Petitto.
Description: New York : Chartwell Books, 2020. | Series: Everyday wellbeing
| Includes index. | Summary: "Straight from the ground and right to your
table, the Plant-Based Cookbook provides delicious and unprocessed
recipes for a delicious, satisfying, whole foods diet"– Provided by
publisher.
Identifiers: LCCN 2020018671 (print) | LCCN 2020018672 (ebook) | ISBN
9780785838593 (hardcover) | ISBN 9780760369494 (ebook)
Subjects: LCSH: Vegetarian cooking. | Seasonal cooking.
Classification: LCC TX837 .P5136 2020 (print) | LCC TX837 (ebook) | DDC
641.5/636–dc23
LC record available at https://lccn.loc.gov/2020018671
LC ebook record available at https://lccn.loc.gov/2020018672

Publisher: Rage Kindelsperger
Creative Director: Laura Drew
Managing Editor: Cara Donaldson
Editor: Leeann Moreau
Cover and Interior Design: Laura Drew
Layout Design: Kim Winscher

Printed in Singapore

THE PLANT-BASED COOKBOOK

100 Delicious Recipes for a Healthy Life

MELISSA PETITTO, R.D.

CHARTWELL
BOOKS

SUMMER RECIPES • 58

FALL RECIPES • 100

SAVORY

SWEET

WINTER RECIPES • 144

PLANT-BASED FOR ALL SEASONS

Eating seasonally is not a new concept; in fact, the notion that we could eat a tomato in January is a modern convenience. In Ayurveda (an ancient Hindu system of diet, herbs, and yoga), the practice of eating seasonally is known as ritucharya. This concept was created so that we ate what was needed during each season to prevent disease and maintain health.

In the spring, we are ready for that first shoot of green to appear. After the chill and snow of winter, seeds push forth from the earth, trees bud, and all of nature awakens. A new energy is sparked within us as well, and we feel the need to venture out and become social again. This is a new beginning, and our bodies crave fresh and lighter fare after the hibernation months. These meals are lush with fresh pastas, asparagus, morels, peas, artichokes, strawberries, lettuces, brothy soups, and simple green salads.

Summer, the season of fresh flowers and plants, grows with us and encourages us to reach our fullest potential. We crave cooling, raw, and room temperature foods to cool our bodies and keep our energy strong. We picnic, we barbeque, and we soak up all the sun we possibly can. These dishes are ripe with perfect juicy summer tomatoes, crispy sun-warmed cucumbers, flawlessly ripened peaches, and juice-laden watermelons. We crave these vegetables and fruits in their simplest forms to showcase their incredible vibrancy.

In autumn, the harvest season, we get to reap the benefits of the spring and summer growth. We gather all of nature's bounty before winter's rest. It is a time to celebrate all that comes with the harvest; warmer foods, slower foods, nutritious back-to-school lunches, and of the inspired Halloween and Thanksgiving recipes. Pumpkins, squashes, mushrooms, beets, pomegranates, and apples are in abundance in these months, and they play a huge role in the holidays of the season.

In the winter, we have completed the cycle and it is time to turn inwards. This period of self-reflection occurs in us as well as in nature. Nature is hibernating. Quiet and withdrawn, she allows her roots to prepare for the upcoming spring. With these cold, dark, and wet days, we crave comfort. We eat foods that help remind us that we will be warm again, such as thick soups, stews, casseroles, and hearty desserts. The holidays of this season are pure decadence, reminding us that food and family and laughter and love are what will replenish us during this time.

I hope you enjoy this cookbook as much as I loved writing it. We truly are so lucky to have nature guide us through the cycle of nourishing our bodies with her abundance. In each chapter of this book you will discover savory and sweet recipes that showcase the bounty of spring, summer, winter, and fall.

SPRING RECIPES

FRUITS & VEGETABLES IN SEASON

Apricots • Artichokes • Asparagus • Belgium Endive • Bitter Melon

Broccoli • Butter Lettuce • Chayote Squash • Cherimoya

Collard Greens • Corn • Fava Beans • Fennel • Fiddlehead Ferns

Green Beans • Honeydew Melon • Jackfruit • Lime • Lychee

Mango • Morel Mushrooms • Mustard Greens • Oranges • Peas

Pineapple • Purple Asparagus • Radicchio • Red Leaf Lettuce

Rhubarb • Snow Peas • Sorrel • Spinach • Strawberries

Swiss Chard • Vidalia Onions • Watercress • White Asparagus

CRISPY CAULIFLOWER BBQ TACOS WITH LIME CREMA AND SHREDDED CABBAGE

SERVES 4

SOY FREE, SUGAR FREE

INGREDIENTS

¾ cup (90 g) brown rice flour

¾ cup (180 ml) unsweetened plain almond milk

¼ cup (60 ml) water

2 teaspoons garlic powder

2 teaspoons paprika

1 cup (100 g) panko breadcrumbs

1 teaspoon sea salt

1 medium head cauliflower, cut into small florets

1 cup (240 ml) habanero pineapple BBQ sauce or other favorite

2 tablespoons (30 ml) sriracha

½ cup (120 g) plain coconut Greek yogurt

2 tablespoons (30 ml) freshly squeezed lime juice

8 corn tortillas

1 cup (110 g) shredded red cabbage

1 avocado, thinly sliced

1 jalapeño, sliced (optional)

Food Fact: Cauliflower is low in calories and high in vitamins C, K, B6, folate, antioxidants, choline, and fiber

These spicy, sweet, crispy, and tangy tacos are so addictive! If you don't like habanero pineapple BBQ sauce, use your favorite one instead. The cauliflower is the only time-consuming part, but if you get all the other ingredients ready while the cauliflower is double baking, these can come together quickly!

METHOD OF PREPARATION

1. Preheat the oven to 350°F (180°C). Line a baking sheet with parchment paper; set aside.

2. In a large bowl, whisk together the flour, milk, water, garlic powder, and paprika.

3. Pour the panko into a shallow bowl or plate and season with the salt.

4. Dip the florets into the batter, making sure they are completely coated. Then roll them in the panko. Lay the coated cauliflower onto the prepared baking sheet. Repeat with all the cauliflower.

5. Transfer the baking sheet to the oven and bake for 25 minutes.

6. Remove from the oven. Pour the BBQ sauce and sriracha into a bowl. Dip the florets into the BBQ sauce mixture. Put them back on the baking sheet. Bake for another 25 minutes.

7. While they are baking, make the lime crema. In a small bowl, whisk together the coconut Greek yogurt and lime juice. Set aside.

8. Warm the tortillas. To serve, top each tortilla with the crispy cauliflower, some red cabbage, sliced avocado, some jalapeño (if using), and a drizzle of the crema.

ITALIAN STUFFED ARTICHOKES

GRAIN FREE, NUT FREE, SOY FREE, SUGAR FREE

INGREDIENTS

4 large globe artichokes

1 cup (100 g) Italian-style breadcrumbs

½ cup (20 g) nutritional yeast

4 cloves garlic, thinly sliced

4 teaspoons (20 ml) extra virgin olive oil

½ teaspoon kosher salt

½ teaspoon freshly cracked black pepper

½ teaspoon Maldon sea salt

Food Fact: Artichokes are cholesterol free, low calorie, fat free, saturated fat free, low sodium, and a good source of dietary fiber, vitamin C, folate, and magnesium

Artichokes are probably my favorite vegetable, and that is saying a lot. I grew up having these Italian stuffed artichokes every year for my birthday; they hold a special place in my heart. They take a little prep work but once stuffed, they are an easy and elegant main dish.

METHOD OF PREPARATION

1. Fill a large stockpot one-fourth of the way with water and bring to a boil over high heat. Insert a steamer. To clean the artichokes, cut about ½ inch (1.3 cm) of the prickly top off and cut the stem so a flat surface remains.

2. Pull the leaves away from the artichoke, creating pockets for stuffing.

3. In a bowl, combine the breadcrumbs, nutritional yeast, and garlic, and then stuff it into the artichoke leaves, making sure to spread the mixture all around.

4. Drizzle with the olive oil and season with the kosher salt and pepper.

5. Place in the steamer basket and cover. Steam over medium heat for 1 hour, checking periodically to make sure the water level does not need to be replenished.

6. When you can easily pull an outside leaf off, they are done. Serve hot with a little Maldon sea salt and a spoon for the heart.

KOREAN SPRING ONION
AND MUNG BEAN PANCAKES

NUT FREE

INGREDIENTS

½ cup (25 g) split mung beans, soaked in
    warm water for 2 hours and drained

1 cup (240 ml) water

1 tablespoon (15 g) brown miso

2 teaspoons coconut sugar

½ cup (60 g) brown rice flour

2 tablespoons (30 ml) grapeseed oil, divided

1 cup (160 g) chopped spring onions

1 cup (120 g) shredded carrot

½ cup (50 g) roughly chopped kimchee

DIPPING SAUCE

3 tablespoons (45 ml) soy sauce

1 teaspoon toasted sesame oil

1 teaspoon coconut sugar

1 teaspoon gochugaru
    (Korean red pepper flakes)

2 teaspoons toasted sesame seeds

Food Fact: Ginger is low in fat,
low in sodium, cholesterol free,
and a good source of vitamin C,
magnesium, and potassium

Spring onions are such a versatile, often
overlooked, vegetable. They get their chance
to shine in this dish. These pancakes are so
tasty, with the combination of carrots, spring
onions, and kimchee. They make a perfect
accompaniment to a miso soup or ginger salad
for a light and simple lunch.

METHOD OF PREPARATION

1. In a high-powered blender, combine the
soaked and drained mung beans, water, miso,
and sugar. Blend on high speed until the mung
beans are finely chopped.

2. Add the brown rice flour and blend on high
speed again until combined, about 20 seconds.
Pour into a large bowl.

3. In a large sauté pan over medium-high heat,
add 2 teaspoons of the grapeseed oil to the pan.
Mound a tablespoon (10 g) each of onions,
carrot, and kimchee in the pan for a pancake,
then top mound with 1 heaping tablespoon
(15 ml) of the batter. Cook the pancakes on one
side for about 2 minutes or until browned and
crispy, then flip and cook on the other side for
another 2 minutes. Transfer to a paper towel-lined
plate and repeat with the remaining oil, onions,
carrots, kimchee, and batter. Keep warm.

4. To make the dipping sauce, whisk together
the soy sauce, oil, sugar, gochugaru, and
sesame seeds in a small bowl. Serve with the
hot pancakes.

GRILLED ASPARAGUS SALAD WITH ARUGULA, MINT, AND OLIVES

SERVES 4

INGREDIENTS

ASPARAGUS

2 pounds (910 g) asparagus, medium thickness, ends trimmed

3 tablespoons (45 ml) olive oil

½ teaspoon sea salt

½ teaspoon freshly ground black pepper

DRESSING

1 tablespoon (11 g) Dijon mustard

1 teaspoon fresh lemon zest

2 tablespoons (30 ml) freshly squeezed lemon juice

1 teaspoon maple syrup

3 tablespoons (45 ml) extra virgin olive oil

¼ teaspoon sea salt

¼ teaspoon freshly ground black pepper

SALAD

4 cups (120 g) wild baby arugula

½ cup (15 g) fresh mint leaves, torn

½ cup (50 g) Cerignola olives, pits removed and roughly chopped

Asparagus has a short window when it is at its peak, and when that season hits, you better believe everything I make has asparagus in it! This salad showcases the flavor of grilled asparagus, something that intensifies and enhances its natural bright, clean, and earthy notes.

METHOD OF PREPARATION

1. Preheat the grill to medium-high. Line a baking sheet with parchment paper.

2. To make the asparagus, spread the spears on the prepared baking sheet. Drizzle with the olive oil and sprinkle with the salt and pepper. Toss to coat.

3. Place the asparagus spears on the grill, making sure they are perpendicular to the grates so that they don't fall through. Cover the grill and grill for 3 to 4 minutes or until nicely charred on one side and still crisp. Do not overcook. Transfer back to the sheet pan.

4. To make the dressing, in a small bowl, whisk together the Dijon, lemon zest, lemon juice, and maple syrup. Slowly drizzle in the olive oil. Season with salt and pepper.

5. To assemble the salad, arrange the grilled asparagus on a platter. Top with the baby arugula, mint leaves, and olives. Drizzle with the dressing and serve.

Food Fact: Asparagus is fat free, saturated fat free, sodium free, cholesterol free, low calorie, a good source of vitamins A and C, and high in folate

COLLARD GREEN WRAPS
WITH TURMERIC RICE, PICKLED VEGGIES,
AND COCONUT PEANUT BUTTER SAUCE SERVES 6

I grew up eating braised collard greens, a cooking method that leaches a lot of the vitamins and nutrients from these naturally healthy greens. This dish showcases their bright and vibrant color and then enhances them with the most beautiful stuffing of yellow turmeric rice and quick pickled spring vegetables, plus the sauce is to die for!

INGREDIENTS

6 large collard green leaves

QUICK PICKLES

1 cup (120 g) carrot matchsticks

1 cup (120 g) daikon radish matchsticks

1 cup (120 g) cucumber matchsticks

1 cup (240 ml) rice vinegar

⅓ cup (65 g) raw cane sugar

1 tablespoon (18 g) sea salt

1 cup (240 ml) hot water

TURMERIC RICE

1 cup (165 g) sprouted brown rice

1 tablespoon (8 g) turmeric

1¾ cups (420 ml) water

½ teaspoon sea salt

1 tablespoon (15 ml) toasted sesame oil

SAUCE

1 cup (240 g) creamy peanut butter

½ cup (120 ml) coconut milk

3 tablespoons (45 ml) water

3 tablespoons (45 ml) freshly squeezed lime juice

3 tablespoons (45 ml) tamari

1 tablespoon (15 ml) sriracha

1 tablespoon (6 g) freshly grated ginger

Food Fact: Collard greens are fat free, cholesterol free, very low sodium, low in calories, a good source of calcium and fiber, and an excellent source of vitamin A, vitamin C, and folate

METHOD OF PREPARATION

1. To make the quick pickles, in three separate mason jars with tight-fitting lids or other glass containers with lids, separate the carrot, daikon, and cucumber. Top each jar with one-third of the vinegar, sugar, salt, and hot water. Close the lids, shake, and allow to pickle while you get the rest of the ingredients ready.

2. To make the rice, in a medium saucepan over medium-high heat, add the rice, turmeric, water, salt, and sesame oil. Stir and bring to a boil. Reduce the heat to a simmer, cover, and cook for 30 minutes. Turn off the heat and allow to steam for another 10 minutes. Fluff with a fork.

3. Cut the protruding stems off of the collard green leaves. Hold a sharp knife parallel to the bottom of the leaf and slice off as much of the tough stem as you can, while maintaining the integrity of the leaf.

4. Bring a large pot of salted water to a boil. Dip each leaf into the water for 20 seconds or until bright green and malleable. Set the blanched greens on a paper towel-lined plate to drain and cool.

5. To make the sauce, in a high-powered blender, combine the peanut butter, coconut milk, water, lime juice, tamari, sriracha, and ginger. Blend on high speed until smooth and creamy. Transfer to a bowl to serve.

6. To make the wraps, lay one collard green leaf face down on a cutting board. Fill the bottom third with 2 tablespoons (30 g) of rice and place the pickled veggies (no brine) on top of the rice. Tuck in the sides and then roll up like a burrito. Repeat with the remaining collards.

7. Serve with the dipping sauce.

LITTLE GEM, CARROT, RADISH, AND SNAP PEA SALAD WITH GREEN GODDESS DRESSING

GLUTEN FREE, GRAIN FREE, NUT FREE, RAW, SOY FREE, UNPROCESSED

INGREDIENTS

DRESSING

1 clove garlic

1 avocado, peeled and pitted

½ cup (120 ml) water

⅓ cup (80 ml) apple cider vinegar

¼ cup (60 ml) freshly squeezed lemon juice

¼ cup (60 ml) extra virgin olive oil

½ cup (20 g) packed basil leaves

½ cup (15 g) packed parsley leaves

½ cup (30 g) packed green onion tops
(green part only)

1 tablespoon (8 g) capers

1 teaspoon raw agave nectar

¼ teaspoon sea salt

SALAD

6 Little Gem lettuce heads, cores removed,
leaves separated

3 colorful heirloom carrots, peeled and shaved

2 watermelon radishes, trimmed and shaved

1 cup (120 g) sugar snap peas, trimmed and
cut on the diagonal

This simple and unique salad should only be made when you have the perfect spring greens, crisp and tender sugar snap peas, luscious and earthy heirloom carrots, and unique and colorful watermelon radishes. The dressing is delicious as a crudité dip too!

METHOD OF PREPARATION

1. To make the dressing, add the garlic, avocado flesh, water, vinegar, lemon juice, oil, basil, parsley, green onions, capers, agave, and salt to a high-powered blender. Blend on high speed for 1 minute or until smooth and creamy. Transfer to a mason jar with a tight-fitting lid.

2. To make the salad, on a platter, arrange the lettuce, carrots, radishes, and sugar snap peas.

3. Drizzle with as much dressing as you like and serve.

Food Fact: Sugar snap peas are an excellent source of vitamin C, and a good source of vitamin K

BLACK RICE RAMEN WITH KOMBU DASHI-MISO BROTH AND SPRING VEGETABLES

SERVES 4

GLUTEN FREE, NUT FREE, SUGAR FREE

Kombu is the key ingredient in making dashi broth. It is a member of the kelp family that provides dishes with umami flavor, nutrients, and minerals. It can even be added to dried beans to make them more digestible. Here we use it to make the base of our miso soup. It takes a few hours to make but is well worth the effort. I make a double batch and freeze the cooled broth for a quick and simple assembly later on. You can add whatever vegetables you want to this soup; it truly is a comfort food.

INGREDIENTS

8 cups (1920 ml) filtered water

4 kombu seaweed squares

One 3-inch (7.5 cm) piece fresh ginger, roughly chopped

4 cloves garlic, smashed

½ cup (30 g) shiitake mushroom stems

¾ cup (180 g) white miso

10 ounces (280 g) dried black rice ramen noodles, cooked according to package directions, drained and reserved

4 teaspoons (20 ml) toasted sesame oil, divided

1 cup (70 g) fresh shiitake mushrooms, stems removed and sliced

4 baby bok choy, stems removed and washed

2 large carrots, peeled and thinly sliced

1 cup (120 g) snow peas, strings removed

1 cup (140 g) fresh peas

Food Fact: Fresh peas are fat free, cholesterol free, sodium free, excellent source of vitamin C, and a good source of vitamin A, folate, and dietary fiber

(continued on page 26)

(continued from page 24)

METHOD OF PREPARATION

1. In a large stockpot over high heat, add the water, kombu, ginger, garlic, and mushroom stems. Bring to a boil, reduce the heat to a simmer, and cook for 3 hours or until flavorful and reduced by half.

2. Drain the solids from the dashi broth and discard. Return the broth back to the stockpot. Whisk in the miso. The broth can be made up to this point, cooled, and frozen for ease. If using right away, cover and keep warm.

3. Divide the noodles among bowls. In a large sauté pan over medium heat, add 1 teaspoon of the oil. When hot, add the mushrooms and sauté for 3 minutes or until tender. Divide the cooked mushrooms among bowls.

4. In the same sauté pan, add another 1 teaspoon of oil. Once hot, add the baby bok choy and sauté for 2 minutes. Divide among the bowls.

5. In the same sauté pan, add 1 teaspoon of oil. Once hot, add the carrots and sauté for 3 minutes or until crisp tender. Divide among the bowls.

6. Lastly, add the remaining 1 teaspoon oil. Once hot, add the snow peas and fresh peas and sauté for 1 minute. Divide among the bowls.

7. To serve, ladle the miso broth over the noodles and vegetables and serve hot.

SPRINGTIME BUDDHA BOWLS WITH CARROT GINGER SAUCE

SERVES 4

NUT FREE

The Buddha bowl is extremely versatile. Here I have showcased the spring farmer's market, but this bowl can be transformed year-round to fit whatever is in abundance. Oh, and you might want to double the dressing; it keeps well for a week in the refrigerator and is great on any and everything.

INGREDIENTS

1¼ cups (200 g) quinoa

1 large sweet potato, peeled and cut into 1-inch (2.5 cm) cubes

5 tablespoons (75 ml) avocado oil, divided

1¼ teaspoons sea salt, divided

4 large heirloom carrots, peeled and cut into 1-inch (2.5 cm) pieces

1 medium golden beet, peeled and cut into 1-inch (2.5 cm) cubes

1 medium red beet, peeled and cut into 1-inch (2.5 cm) cubes

2 cups (140 g) broccoli florets

1 pound (455 g) asparagus, ends trimmed

2 cups (60 g) spring baby greens

2 ripe avocados, halved, pitted, and thinly sliced before serving

2 Persian cucumbers, thinly sliced

SAUCE

2 large carrots, peeled and roughly chopped

One 2-inch (5 cm) piece fresh ginger, peeled and roughly chopped

⅓ cup (80 ml) rice vinegar

⅓ cup (80 ml) extra virgin olive oil

1½ tablespoons (23 ml) maple syrup

2 tablespoons (30 ml) freshly squeezed lime juice

1 tablespoon (15 ml) tamari

1 tablespoon (15 ml) sriracha

2 teaspoons toasted sesame oil

Food Fact: Broccoli is low fat, saturated fat free, low sodium, cholesterol free, high in vitamin C and folate, and a good source of dietary fiber and potassium

(continued on page 28)

(continued from page 27)

METHOD OF PREPARATION

1. Cook the quinoa according to the package directions. Set aside and keep warm.

2. Preheat the oven to 425°F (220°C). Line three baking sheets with parchment paper; set aside.

3. In a large bowl, add the sweet potato, drizzle with 1 tablespoon (15 ml) of the oil, and sprinkle with ¼ teaspoon of the salt. Transfer to one of the baking sheets, arranging in a single layer on half of the baking sheet.

4. In the same bowl, add the carrots, drizzle with 1 tablespoon (15 ml) of oil and sprinkle with ¼ teaspoon of salt. Toss well to coat and arrange in a single layer on the other half of the baking sheet. Transfer to the oven and roast for 30 minutes or until tender and caramelized, stirring halfway through the cooking time.

5. In the same bowl, add the golden and red beets, drizzle with 1 tablespoon (15 ml) of olive oil and sprinkle with the ¼ teaspoon of salt. Toss to coat and add to the second baking sheet. Transfer to the oven and roast for 25 to 30 minutes or until tender, stirring halfway through the cooking time.

6. In the same bowl, add the broccoli, drizzle with 1 tablespoon (15 ml) of olive oil, sprinkle with ¼ teaspoon salt, and arrange on half of the third baking sheet.

7. Finally, add the asparagus to the same bowl, drizzle with the remaining 1 tablespoon (15 ml) olive oil, sprinkle with the remaining ¼ teaspoon salt, and arrange on the other half of the third baking sheet. Transfer to the oven and roast for 10 to 15 minutes, stirring halfway through.

8. While the vegetables are roasting, make the sauce. In a high-speed blender, add the carrots, ginger, rice vinegar, olive oil, maple syrup, lime juice, tamari, sriracha, and sesame oil. Blend on high speed for 1 to 2 minutes or until smooth and creamy.

9. To serve, divide the quinoa among four bowls. Divide all the roasted vegetables among the bowls. Divide the spring greens, avocado, and sliced cucumbers among the bowls. Drizzle with the sauce and serve at room temperature or hot.

CREAM OF CELERY AND CELERY ROOT SOUP

SERVES 4

GLUTEN FREE, GRAIN FREE, NUT FREE, RAW, SOY FREE, SUGAR FREE

INGREDIENTS

¼ cup (60 g) vegan butter, such as Miyoko's

1 large head celery, washed and thinly sliced, leaves reserved for garnish

1 medium leek, washed well and sliced

8 ounces (225 g) celery root, peeled and diced

8 ounces (225 g) Yukon gold potatoes, peeled and diced

4 cloves garlic, minced

4 cups (960 ml) vegetable broth

½ cup (15 g) chopped fresh parsley

½ to 1 teaspoon sea salt

½ teaspoon freshly ground black pepper

¼ cup (15 g) fresh chervil leaves

Food Fact: Yukon gold potatoes are fat free, saturated fat free, cholesterol free, low in sodium, excellent source of vitamin C, and a good source of potassium

Celery and celery root often get thought of as an understudy and not the star, but not in this soup. This light and flavorful soup is so comforting and refreshing. Pair it with a salad or a chunk of great crusty bread and you have a simple lunch or a light dinner.

METHOD OF PREPARATION

1. Heat the butter in a large Dutch oven over medium heat. Add the celery, leek, celery root, and potatoes. Sauté for 10 minutes, stirring frequently, until softened and lightly caramelized.

2. Add the garlic and stir for 30 seconds.

3. Add the broth and turn the heat up to medium-high. Bring to a boil, lower the heat to a simmer and cook for another 10 minutes or until the celery root and potato are tender.

4. Add the parsley and stir.

5. Using an immersion blender, blend the soup until creamy. Season with salt and pepper.

6. Ladle into bowls and serve topped with the reserved celery leaves and chervil.

FRESH PASTA WITH MORELS AND PEAS

GRAIN FREE, NUT FREE, SOY FREE, SUGAR FREE

Traditional homemade pasta normally uses egg yolks; I promise you won't feel like this one is missing a thing! It's so versatile as well. You can use it for lasagna noodles, pappardelle, fettuccine, linguine, or spaghetti. Morels can be a little sandy, so make sure you take a damp cloth to them and brush them off well. If these little sponges do need to be rinsed because they are particularly dirty, make sure you dry them extremely well on a kitchen towel prior to cooking, or you will just steam them and miss the caramelization we are looking for in this dish.

INGREDIENTS

FRESH PASTA

2 cups (240 g) semolina flour, plus more for sprinkling

1 cup (120 g) all-purpose flour

1 cup (240 ml) hot water

Food Fact: Morels are fat free, saturated fat free, cholesterol free, low in sodium, a good source of manganese and phosphorous, and an excellent source of vitamin D, copper, and iron

SAUCE

¼ cup (60 g) vegan butter

4 ounces (112 g) morels, cleaned with a damp cloth, cut into quarters lengthwise

4 cloves garlic, minced

1 cup (140 g) fresh shelled peas

¼ cup (10 g) nutritional yeast

½ to 1 teaspoon sea salt

1 teaspoon freshly ground black pepper

Dill (for garnish)

(continued on page 36)

(continued from page 34)

METHOD OF PREPARATION

1. To make the pasta, in the bowl of a food processor, combine the semolina and all-purpose flour. Blend on high speed, slowly adding the hot water through the spout. The mixture will start out coarse, then slowly form one big ball of dough after about 2 minutes of processing. Continue processing for 30 seconds after a ball has formed.

2. Remove the dough from the processor. Flatten it into a disk ½ inch (1.3 cm) thick, cut it into quarters, then cover with a dry towel and allow to rest for 15 minutes.

3. Sprinkle a little extra semolina flour onto a clean work surface. Roll out of one of the quarters of dough to the desired thickness, between ⅛ and ¼ inch (3 and 6 mm). Cut into desired shapes. For this pasta, fettuccine or spaghetti would be ideal.

4. Bring a large pot of salted water to a boil. Boil the pasta for 2 to 3 minutes. Reserve 1 cup (240 ml) of the cooking liquid and drain the pasta.

5. While the pasta is cooking, heat a large sauté pan over medium heat. Add the butter and melt. Add the morels and cook for 3 to 4 minutes, until lightly browned. Stir in the garlic and peas and sauté for 1 minute longer.

6. Add the nutritional yeast, salt, and pepper. Turn the heat to low.

7. Add the cooked pasta to the sauce, along with the reserved cooking liquid. Sauté for 30 seconds to meld the flavors, garnish with dill, and then serve immediately.

STRAWBERRY SHORTCAKE
WITH WHIPPED COCONUT CREAM

GRAIN FREE, SOY FREE

Strawberries are like candy when they are in season. They are sugary sweet and vibrant in color. Any other time I could care less about this nutritious fruit, but at their peak, I cannot get enough. Make this simple dish when you have that feeling, because any other time and it's just not worth it.

INGREDIENTS

WHIPPED COCONUT CREAM
One 14-ounce (392 g) can coconut cream, chilled overnight

2 tablespoons (16 g) organic powdered sugar

1 teaspoon vanilla extract

STRAWBERRIES
2 pints (455 g each) strawberries, rinsed

½ cup (100 g) coconut sugar

Food Fact: Strawberries are fat free, saturated fat free, sodium free, cholesterol free, and are high in vitamin C and folate

BISCUITS
4 cups (480 g) unbleached all-purpose flour

3 tablespoons (36 g) organic unbleached cane sugar

¼ teaspoon kosher salt

5 teaspoons (15 g) baking powder

1 cup (240 g) vegan butter, such as Miyoko's, at room temperature, divided

1¼ cups (300 ml) cashew or almond cream

Sprig of mint (for garnish)

(continued on page 38)

(continued from page 37)

METHOD OF PREPARATION

1. To make the whipped coconut cream, place your mixing bowl in the freezer for 10 minutes.

2. Once your bowl is cold, remove the can of cold coconut milk from the refrigerator. Carefully remove the top of the can; do not shake or tip upside down. Scoop the thick layer of coconut cream from the top of the can, leaving the water at the bottom for another use.

3. Using a whisk attachment, beat the coconut cream on medium speed for 2 to 4 minutes, or until the cream becomes light and fluffy and peaks form. Add the powdered sugar and vanilla and beat until just incorporated.

4. To prepare the strawberries, hull the strawberries and cut them into quarters. Place half in a bowl with the coconut sugar and lightly mash. Cover and set aside to let the flavors meld. Reserve the other half of the strawberries in a bowl.

5. To make the biscuits, preheat the oven to 450°F (230°C). Line a baking sheet with parchment paper; set aside.

6. In a large bowl, sift the flour, cane sugar, salt, and baking powder. Whisk to combine. Add ¾ cup (180 g) of the butter and rub it into the dry ingredients until well dispersed and crumbly.

7. Add the cashew or almond cream and mix to form a soft dough.

8. Drop 8 round mounds onto the prepared baking sheet, spacing them about 2 inches (5 cm) apart.

9. Melt the remaining ¼ cup (60 g) butter and brush the tops of the drop biscuits.

10. Transfer to the oven and bake for 15 minutes or until the tops are golden brown and puffy. Allow to cool for 5 minutes.

11. To serve, cut the biscuits in half. Place the bottom halves on a platter, spoon a large dollop of the coconut cream among the four bottom halves, continue with a large dollop of the mashed strawberries and quartered strawberries among the biscuit bottoms. Then finish with the top half of the biscuit and a final dollop of strawberries and cream. Garnish with mint and serve immediately.

COCONUT RICE PUDDING WITH MANGO

GLUTEN FREE, SOY FREE

INGREDIENTS

1½ cups (240 g) forbidden or black rice

Two 14-ounce (392 g) cans unsweetened light coconut milk

½ teaspoon sea salt

½ cup (100 g) organic unbleached sugar or coconut sugar

½ vanilla bean, split open and scraped

1 cup (240 ml) nut milk

1 lime, juiced

2 ripe mangoes, peeled, pitted, and diced

Food Fact: Mangos are low fat, saturated fat free, sodium free, cholesterol free, high in vitamin A, and a good source of vitamin C

Rice pudding: it's such a shockingly delightful dessert to me. This one is so creamy and complex, and exquisitely beautiful. The mango on top of this coconut-laden black rice is just perfect. I always serve a little extra diced mango with this pudding. Someone always wants just a little more of its goodness.

METHOD OF PREPARATION

1. Mix the rice, coconut milk, salt, sugar, and vanilla bean in a large pot; bring to a boil. Decrease the heat to low and simmer, stirring occasionally, for 1 hour or until the mixture reaches the desired thickness and the rice is done.

2. Add the nut milk during the last ½ hour of cooking and stir more frequently to prevent scorching, as the pudding will absorb most of the liquid. Remove from the heat and add the lime juice to taste.

3. Taste for salt and adjust as desired.

4. Let cool and serve with diced mango tossed with the remaining lime juice to taste.

STRAWBERRY COCONUT MILKSHAKE

GRAIN FREE, NUT FREE, RAW, SOY FREE

INGREDIENTS

2 medium bananas, peeled, sliced, and frozen

One 14.5-ounce (406 g) can coconut milk

1 cup (145 g) fresh strawberries, hulled and frozen

2 tablespoons (30 ml) maple syrup

1 teaspoon vanilla extract

One trick I have learned over the years of eating with the seasons is that if I love a fruit and it has a short window of being the most nutritious and tasty, I individually quick-freeze them so that I can have them at other times of the year. Berries are ideal to be used in this way. Just wash your berries and hull/chop them if necessary, place them on a parchment-covered baking sheet, transfer to the freezer, and freeze them. Then store in an airtight container in the freezer until you need them. That way, you can have this refreshing milkshake any time of the year.

METHOD OF PREPARATION

1. In a high-powered blender, combine the frozen bananas and coconut milk. Blend on high speed until smooth and creamy, about 1 minute.

2. Add the strawberries, maple syrup, and vanilla. Blend on high speed until smooth and creamy, about 1 minute longer.

3. Pour into two glasses and serve immediately.

KEY LIME PIE SHAKE

GRAIN FREE, SOY FREE

INGREDIENTS

2 medium bananas, peeled, sliced,
   and frozen

1 cup (240 g) plain almond Greek yogurt

2 teaspoons finely grated Key lime zest

1 cup (240 ml) freshly squeezed Key
   lime juice

¼ cup (60 ml) coconut nectar

1 teaspoon vanilla extract

2 lime wedges

2 tablespoons (10 g) vegan graham
   cracker crumbs

Food Fact: Limes are fat free,
saturated fat free, sodium
free, cholesterol free, low
calorie, and high in vitamin C

Key lime pie is such a treat, one that is traditionally not plant-based friendly. This shake is super easy, so flavorful, and wonderfully reminiscent of the actual pie. I do not suggest substituting regular limes for the Key limes; it's just not as good. And make sure you do not skip the graham cracker-rimmed glass; it sets this shake over the top.

METHOD OF PREPARATION

1. In a high-speed blender, combine the bananas, yogurt, zest, juice, coconut nectar, and vanilla. Blend on high speed until smooth and creamy, about 1 minute.

2. To serve, rub the lime wedges along the rim of two glasses, then roll the rim in the graham cracker crumbs. Pour the shake into the glass and serve with the lime wedges immediately.

CARROT CAKE
WITH CREAM CHEESE FROSTING

SERVES 16

GRAIN FREE

Carrot cake happens to be my favorite cake, and this one is so moist and tender from the pineapple. Make sure you line the cake pans with parchment, which ensures easy removal from the pans.

INGREDIENTS

CAKE

Coconut oil spray

1¼ cups (300 g) unsweetened applesauce

2 cups (400 g) coconut sugar

9 tablespoons (135 ml) aquafaba
(chickpea water)

1 cup (120 g) unbleached all-purpose flour

1 cup (120 g) almond flour

1½ teaspoons baking powder

1 teaspoon baking soda

½ teaspoon kosher salt

1 teaspoon ground cinnamon

2 cups (240 g) freshly grated carrot

1 cup (100 g) shredded unsweetened coconut

1 cup (240 g) crushed pineapple in juice,
do not drain

FROSTING

½ cup (120 g) vegan butter, such as Miyoko's,
at room temperature

8 ounces (225 g) vegan cream cheese,
at room temperature

1 teaspoon vanilla extract

3 cups (360 g) organic powdered sugar

TOPPING (OPTIONAL)

1 cup (140 g) toasted, chopped walnuts

1 cup (100 g) toasted shredded coconut

METHOD OF PREPARATION

1. Preheat the oven to 350°F (180°C). Line two 9-inch (23 cm) cake pans with parchment paper and coat with coconut oil spray; set aside.

2. To make the cake, in a large bowl, combine the applesauce, coconut sugar, and aquafaba. Whisk to blend.

3. In another large bowl, whisk together the flour, almond flour, baking powder, baking soda, salt, and cinnamon. Add the dry ingredients to the wet ingredients and stir to combine.

4. Add the carrots, coconut, and crushed pineapple to the mixture and stir until just combined. Divide the mixture between the prepared pans and transfer to the oven.

5. Bake for 35 to 40 minutes or until a toothpick inserted in the center comes out clean.

6. Let the cakes cool for 10 minutes before removing from the pans and cooling completely on a wire rack.

7. While the cake is baking, make the frosting. In a large bowl with a handheld mixer or in the bowl of a stand mixer, combine the softened butter and cream cheese. Whisk on medium speed until combined. Add the vanilla.

8. Slowly incorporate the powdered sugar until the frosting is smooth and creamy.

9. To frost the cake, invert one cake on a cake stand or platter. Apply half of the frosting and spread. Add the other cake on top and spread the other half of the frosting over it. Add the toasted walnuts and/or coconut, if desired. Refrigerate for at least 1 hour prior to serving.

LEMON POUND CAKE
WITH FRESH SPRING BERRIES

GRAIN FREE, SOY FREE

INGREDIENTS

Coconut oil spray

3½ cups (420 g) unbleached all-purpose flour

¼ cup (30 g) cornstarch

2½ tablespoons (20 g) baking powder

½ teaspoon kosher salt

3 tablespoons (18 g) freshly grated lemon zest

¼ cup (60 ml) freshly squeezed lemon juice

2 cups (200 g) organic unbleached cane sugar

⅔ cup (160 ml) coconut oil, melted

1⅔ cups (400 ml) unsweetened almond or
    cashew milk

2 tablespoons (30 g) unsweetened applesauce

1 teaspoon vanilla extract

1 teaspoon lemon extract

2 cups (300 g) mixed fresh berries, such
    as blueberries, strawberries, blackberries,
    raspberries, and/or boysenberries

Food Fact: Blackberries are
good for your brain, and
are high in antioxidants
and vitamins C, K, and A

Pound cake by definition is a cake that contains equal weights of flour, butter, and sugar… whoa! This lightened-up version is charmingly refreshing with the lemon flavor and then made even more so with a bounty of berries. This recipe makes two loaf cakes or one large cake, but it freezes well.

METHOD OF PREPARATION

1. Preheat the oven to 350°F (180°C). Spray two 8½ x 4½ x 2½-inch (21.6 x 11.4 x 6.3 cm) loaf pans or one Bundt pan with coconut spray; set aside.

2. In a large bowl, whisk together the flour, cornstarch, baking powder, and salt.

3. In another large bowl, whisk together the lemon zest, lemon juice, sugar, coconut oil, nut milk, applesauce, vanilla, and lemon extract.

4. Add the wet ingredients to the dry and whisk until just combined. Do not overmix.

5. Divide the batter between the prepared loaf pans and transfer to the oven. Bake for 45 minutes to 1 hour or until a toothpick inserted in the center comes out clean.

6. Remove from the oven and allow to cool in the pan for 10 minutes. Turn the cakes out onto a wire rack and cool until ready to slice.

7. To serve, wash and prepare all the berries. Hull and quarter the strawberries, if using.

8. Slice the pound cake and serve with a big spoonful of fresh berries.

COCONUT BREAD

GRAIN FREE, SOY FREE

INGREDIENTS

Coconut oil spray

1½ cups (180 g) almond flour

1 cup (120 g) whole spelt flour

1¼ cups (125 g) unsweetened
   shredded coconut

2 teaspoons baking powder

½ teaspoon baking soda

½ teaspoon freshly grated nutmeg

½ teaspoon kosher salt

One 13.5-ounce (378 g) can full-fat
   coconut milk

¼ cup (60 ml) coconut oil, melted

¼ cup (60 ml) coconut nectar

1 teaspoon vanilla extract

This quadruple-threat coconut bread—with coconut milk, coconut oil, shredded coconut, and coconut nectar—is perfect toasted with some nut butter for breakfast or a snack or topped with some whipped coconut cream (page 34) for dessert. It freezes well too, so make a double batch and have it ready for whenever the craving hits.

METHOD OF PREPARATION

1. Preheat the oven to 350°F (180°C). Spray an 8½ x 4½ x 2½-inch (21.6 x 11.4 x 6.3 cm) loaf pan with coconut spray; set aside.

2. In a large mixing bowl, whisk together the almond flour, spelt flour, shredded coconut, baking powder, baking soda, nutmeg, and salt. Make a well in the center of the dry ingredients.

3. In another large bowl, whisk together the coconut milk, coconut oil, coconut nectar, and vanilla.

4. Add the wet ingredients to the well in the center of the dry ingredients and use a wooden spoon to stir until just combined. Do not overmix.

5. Transfer to the prepared pan and bake for 40 to 45 minutes or until a toothpick inserted in the center comes out clean and the bread is golden brown.

6. Remove from the oven and cool in the pan for 10 minutes. Turn out onto a wire rack and cool completely before slicing.

BAKED LEMON POPPY SEED DOUGHNUTS

GLUTEN FREE, GRAIN FREE, SOY FREE

These pretty little doughnuts are just bursting with lemon flavor. The extra step of the poppy seed drizzle sets these baked doughnuts over the top. These are a quick bread, so do not overmix the batter or you will have hockey pucks instead of light and airy doughnuts.

INGREDIENTS

DOUGHNUTS

Coconut oil spray

2¼ cups (270 g) oat flour

½ cup (60 g) finely ground almond flour

1 tablespoon (6 g) poppy seeds

1 teaspoon baking soda

½ teaspoon baking powder

¼ teaspoon kosher salt

½ cup + 2 tablespoons (150 ml) warm water

½ cup (120 ml) unsweetened almond milk, at room temperature

2 tablespoons (30 ml) freshly squeezed lemon juice

2 tablespoons (12 g) lemon zest

3 tablespoons (45 ml) coconut oil, melted

¼ cup (50 g) coconut sugar

¼ cup (60 ml) maple syrup

1 teaspoon vanilla extract

GLAZES

½ cup (60 g) organic powdered sugar, divided

1½ teaspoons lemon juice

1 teaspoon unsweetened almond milk

1 teaspoon poppy seeds

Food Fact: Lemons are fat free, saturated fat free, sodium free, cholesterol free, low calorie, and are high in vitamin C

(continued on page 52)

(continued from page 50)

METHOD OF PREPARATION

1. Preheat the oven to 350°F (180°C). Spray two doughnut pans with coconut oil; set aside.

2. To make the doughnuts, in a large bowl, whisk together the oat flour, almond flour, poppy seeds, baking soda, baking powder, and salt.

3. In another medium bowl, whisk together the water, milk, lemon juice, lemon zest, coconut oil, coconut sugar, maple syrup, and vanilla.

4. Add the wet ingredients to the dry and whisk until just incorporated. Do not overmix.

5. Divide the batter between the prepared doughnut pans. Tap the pans to release any air bubbles. Transfer to the oven and bake for 10 to 14 minutes or until a toothpick inserted near the center comes out clean.

6. Allow to cool on a rack for 10 minutes. Tap the pans on a flat surface to loosen the doughnuts and then flip the pan upside down to release the doughnuts. Allow to cool completely on the wire rack.

7. While the doughnuts are cooling, make the glazes. In a small bowl, combine ¼ cup (30 g) of the powdered sugar and lemon juice. Whisk until combined. In another small bowl, whisk together the remaining ¼ cup (30 g) powdered sugar, almond milk, and poppy seeds.

8. Dip the doughnuts in the lemon glaze and then drizzle with the poppy glaze. Transfer back to the wire rack to allow the glaze to firm up.

MATCHA SPONGE CAKE WITH RASPBERRY CREAM

SERVES 8

GRAIN FREE, NUT FREE, SOY FREE

A sponge cake is a batter traditionally made with air being beaten into separated egg yolks and whites. This plant-based twist uses aquafaba beaten to form soft white peaks and is equally light and airy. If you can't find self-rising flour, another key ingredient in this cake, simply mix 2 cups (240 g) all purpose flour + 1 tablespoon (8 g) baking powder + ½ teaspoon kosher salt, then measure out 1½ cups (180 g) for this recipe.

INGREDIENTS

CAKE

Coconut oil spray

1 cup (240 g) unsweetened plain coconut yogurt

¾ cup (150 g) organic cane sugar

1 teaspoon baking soda

½ teaspoon baking powder

½ cup (120 ml) aquafaba (chickpea water)

½ cup (120 ml) coconut oil, melted

1 teaspoon vanilla extract

1½ teaspoons high-quality matcha powder

½ teaspoon kosher salt

1½ cups (180 g) self-rising flour

FROSTING

One 13.5-ounce (378 g) can full-fat coconut milk, refrigerated overnight

2 tablespoons (30 g) seedless raspberry jam (or fresh raspberries)

1 teaspoon of lime zest (optional)

Food Fact: Raspberries are fat free, saturated fat free, cholesterol free, and high in dietary fiber and vitamin C

(continued on page 54)

(continued from page 53)

METHOD OF PREPARATION

1. Preheat the oven to 350°F (180°C). Spray two 8-inch (20 cm) cake pans with coconut oil, line with parchment paper, and set aside.

2. To make the cake, in a large bowl, combine the coconut yogurt, sugar, baking soda, and baking powder. Allow to sit for 10 minutes or until small bubbles start to form.

3. While the coconut mixture is working, whip the aquafaba. In another large bowl, use an electric mixer on high speed to create soft, white peaks, 5 to 10 minutes. Set aside.

4. Once you see bubbles in the yogurt mixture, whisk in the coconut oil, vanilla, matcha powder, and salt. Then sift the flour over the top of the mixture and fold it in. The batter will be stiff at this point.

5. Fold half of the aquafaba into the batter at a time, until your batter is light and airy.

6. Divide the batter between the prepared pans and transfer to the oven. Bake for 20 to 30 minutes or until a toothpick inserted in the center comes out clean.

7. Allow the cakes to cool completely on a wire rack. Once cool, invert the pans and remove the cakes from the pans.

8. To make the frosting, open the can of coconut milk, being careful not to shake it. You want just the cream, not the coconut water. Scoop off the cream, leaving the water behind for another use, and transfer to a medium bowl. Using an electric mixer on medium-high speed, whip the coconut cream until light and fluffy, 3 to 5 minutes.

9. Once the cakes have cooled completely, place one round on a cake stand and spread or pipe with half of the raspberry. Option to instead add whole raspberries, in two circular rings on top of the layer of cream, as pictured. Add the other cake on top and decorate with fresh raspberries and lime zest. Best eaten within 2 days.

BLUEBERRY COFFEE CAKE

GRAIN FREE, SOY FREE

INGREDIENTS

Coconut oil spray

1 cup (120 g) unbleached all-purpose flour

½ cup (60 g) oat flour

6 tablespoons (75 g) coconut brown sugar

2 teaspoons baking powder

½ teaspoon kosher salt

½ teaspoon ground cinnamon

6 tablespoons (90 ml) aquafaba
(chickpea water), lightly whipped (see page 54)

⅓ cup (80 g) unsweetened applesauce

½ cup (120 ml) unsweetened almond
or cashew milk

1 teaspoon vanilla extract

1 cup (150 g) fresh blueberries

TOPPING

⅓ cup (40 g) oat flour

3 tablespoons (36 g) coconut brown sugar

½ teaspoon ground cinnamon

¼ cup (60 ml) coconut oil

⅓ cup (45 g) walnuts, chopped

Food Fact: Blueberries are low
fat, saturated fat free, sodium free,
cholesterol free, and a good source
of dietary fiber and vitamin C

A simple coffee cake is a thing of beauty; is it breakfast, a snack, or dessert? Who knows! What we do know is it is delicious. You could switch up the blueberries for blackberries, raspberries, or boysenberries. Do not overmix this quick bread!

METHOD OF PREPARATION

1. Preheat the oven to 350°F (180°C). Spray a 9 x 9-inch (23 x 23 cm) pan with coconut oil; set aside.

2. In a large bowl, whisk together the flour, oat flour, coconut sugar, baking powder, salt, and cinnamon.

3. In another medium bowl, whisk together the aquafaba, applesauce, milk, and vanilla.

4. Add the wet ingredients to the dry and whisk until just incorporated. Do not overmix. Fold in the blueberries.

5. Pour the batter into the prepared pan.

6. To make the topping, in a small bowl, combine the oat flour, brown sugar, cinnamon, oil, and walnuts. Mix until crumbly.

7. Scatter the mixture over the top of the batter. Transfer to the oven and bake for 25 to 30 minutes or until a toothpick inserted in the center comes out clean.

8. Serve warm.

SUMMER
RECIPES

FRUITS & VEGETABLES IN SEASON

Anaheim Chile • Apricots • Armenian Cucumbers • Asian Pear

Beets • Bell Peppers • Black Currants • Blackberries • Blueberries

Butter Lettuce • Cantaloupe • Casaba Melon • Champagne Grapes

Chayote Squash • Cherries • Chinese Long Beans • Corn

Crenshaw Melon • Crookneck Squash • Cucumbers • Durian

Eggplant • Elderberries • Endive • French Beans • Figs

Galia Melon • Grape Tomatoes • Grapefruit • Grapes • Green Beans

Green Soybeans • Hearts of Palm • Honeydew Melons • Jackfruit

Jalapeño Peppers • Key Limes • Lima Beans • Limes • Lychees

Mulberries • Nectarines • Okra • Passion Fruit • Peaches • Peas

Persian Melon • Plums • Radishes • Raspberries • Shallots

Sugar Snap Peas • Summer Squash • Tomatillos • Tomatoes

Watermelon • Yukon Gold Potatoes • Zucchini

CRISPY CORN FRITTERS
WITH TARRAGON REMOULADE

GLUTEN FREE, SOY FREE

These are super simple to make and oh so delicious! These fritters are best when corn is in season and incredibly sweet, but if you have a craving for them in the winter, frozen and thawed corn comes in a close second. The remoulade is equally fantastic and keeps well for a week or so in the refrigerator. I dare you to eat just one of these; they will be gone as quickly as you can make them.

INGREDIENTS

REMOULADE

1½ cups (210 g) raw cashews, soaked in room
   temperature water for 2+ hours, drained, and rinsed

½ cup (120 ml) water

½ cup (120 ml) pickle juice

2 tablespoons (30 ml) freshly squeezed lemon juice

1 tablespoon (15 ml) hot sauce

1 clove garlic

2 teaspoons stone-ground mustard

½ teaspoon sea salt

½ cup (50 g) minced green onion

½ cup (100 g) pickle relish

¼ cup (16 g) chopped fresh tarragon

Food Fact: Corn is low fat, saturated fat free, sodium free, cholesterol free, and a good source of vitamin C

FRITTERS

3 cups (450 g) fresh corn kernels
   (may use frozen if fresh isn't available)

¼ cup (4 g) chopped fresh cilantro

¼ cup (25 g) chopped green onions

1 jalapeño, seeded and minced

Juice of ½ lime

1 cup (120 g) brown rice flour

1 teaspoon baking powder

½ teaspoon sea salt

¼ teaspoon freshly ground black pepper

½ teaspoon chili powder

⅓ cup (80 ml) aquafaba (chickpea water),
   lightly whipped (see page 54)

¼ cup (60 ml) unsweetened nut milk

1 cup (120 g) shredded nut cheese (optional)

2 tablespoons (30 ml) avocado oil, divided

METHOD OF PREPARATION

1. Make the remoulade ahead of time and allow to fuse flavors in the refrigerator while you make the fritters. In a high-powered blender, combine the soaked and cashews, water, pickle juice, lemon juice, hot sauce, garlic, mustard, and salt. Blend on high speed until smooth and creamy.

2. Transfer to a bowl or mason jar and stir in the green onions, pickle relish, and tarragon. Cover and refrigerate until needed.

3. To make the fritters, place the corn in a large bowl and add the cilantro, green onions, jalapeño, and lime juice. Stir to combine.

4. In a separate medium bowl, whisk together the flour, baking powder, salt, black pepper, and chili powder.

5. Add the dry ingredients to the corn mixture and stir to combine.

6. Add the whipped aquafaba, nut milk, and cheese (if using) to the corn mixture and stir to combine. The batter will be thick.

7. In a large pan over medium heat, add a drizzle of the oil. Once hot, scoop a generous spoonful of the batter into the hot oil. Press the batter down with the back of a spatula. Fry for 2 to 3 minutes per side or until you see the edges turn brown and crispy. Turn the fritters over and cook for another 2 to 3 minutes on the second side. Transfer to a baking sheet lined with paper towels and repeat with the remaining oil and batter.

8. Serve the fritters warm with the remoulade.

PERFECT SUMMER HEIRLOOM TOMATO-WATERMELON SALAD WITH CRISP BASIL AND AGED BALSAMIC

SERVES 4

GLUTEN FREE, GRAIN FREE, NUT FREE, SOY FREE, SUGAR FREE, UNPROCESSED

INGREDIENTS

1½ cups (90 g) fresh basil leaves

Olive oil spray

½ teaspoon kosher salt

4 heirloom tomatoes, different colors

2 cups (300 g) cubed baby seedless watermelon in 1-inch (2.5 cm) cubes

2 tablespoons (30 ml) extra virgin olive oil

1½ tablespoons (23 ml) good-quality aged balsamic

1 teaspoon Maldon sea salt

¾ teaspoon freshly ground black pepper

Food Fact: Tomatoes are low fat, saturated fat free, very low sodium, cholesterol free, low calorie, high in vitamins A and C, and a good source of potassium

One of my favorite childhood memories is going out to our backyard garden in the middle of summer, barefoot with a saltshaker in hand, picking a sun-warmed ripe tomato off the vine, and gobbling it down like an apple, salting every bite. Make this simple salad when tomatoes are in abundance and watermelon is crispy and sweet. This cooling salad will be a favorite at every outdoor event and BBQ.

METHOD OF PREPARATION

1. Preheat the oven to 325°F (170°C). Line a baking sheet with parchment paper.

2. Arrange the basil leaves on the prepared baking sheet, mist with olive oil spray, and sprinkle with the kosher salt. Toss to coat and make sure they are in a single layer.

3. Transfer to the oven and bake for 5 to 10 minutes. Check after 5 minutes. They should be dark brown and crispy. Remove from the oven and allow to cool.

4. Wash the tomatoes, core them, and cut them into bite-size pieces. Arrange on a large platter.

5. Add the watermelon cubes to the platter.

6. Drizzle with the olive oil and balsamic and season with the Maldon sea salt and pepper, and sprinkle with the crispy basil leaves.

CARAMELIZED GOLDEN TOMATO TARTE TATIN

SERVES 8

GRAIN FREE, NUT FREE, SOY FREE

This tart is so elegant and equally easy to make. I love to serve this at a picnic at room temperature or at a family Sunday dinner, warm. The flaky pastry, sweet caramelized yellow tomatoes, and salty kalamata olives come together perfectly for a beautiful summer side or an elegant main dish. The cast-iron skillet is the secret to this dish turning out just so!

INGREDIENTS

One 14-ounce (392 g) package vegan puff pastry, thawed

2 tablespoons (30 ml) olive oil

1 sweet onion, halved and thinly sliced

¼ cup (60 ml) water, divided

¼ cup (50 g) raw cane sugar

½ teaspoon sherry vinegar

¼ cup (25 g) pitted kalamata olives, roughly chopped

1 pound (455 g) yellow grape tomatoes

½ teaspoon sea salt

½ teaspoon freshly ground black pepper

½ cup (30 g) basil leaves, cut into chiffonade

METHOD OF PREPARATION

1. Preheat the oven to 425°F (220°C).

2. Unroll the puff pastry, cut out a 10-inch (25 cm) circle, cover, and chill until ready to use.

3. In a cast-iron skillet over medium heat, add the olive oil, onions, and 2 tablespoons (30 ml) of the water and cook, stirring frequently, until the onions are golden and caramelized, about 20 minutes. Transfer to a bowl.

4. To make a simple caramel: In the same skillet, add the remaining 2 tablespoons (30 ml) water and sugar and cook over medium heat, swirling the pan gently without stirring, until the sugar melts and turns amber, 7 to 10 minutes. Add the vinegar and swirl gently.

5. Sprinkle the chopped olives over the caramel. Scatter the tomatoes over the olives and then sprinkle with the caramelized onions. Season with the salt and pepper.

6. Top with the chilled puff pastry, tucking the edges into the pan and cutting four long vents into the top of the pastry.

7. Transfer the skillet to the oven and bake for 30 minutes or until the tart is golden and puffed. Remove from the oven and let stand for 5 minutes.

8. Run a knife around the edges to loosen the pastry from the pan, flip the tart out onto a serving platter, and cut into 8 wedges. Sprinkle with the basil and serve immediately.

GRILLED CAULIFLOWER STEAKS WITH OLIVE-PEPPER-HERB SALSA

SERVES 4

GLUTEN FREE, GRAIN FREE, NUT FREE, SOY FREE, SUGAR FREE, UNPROCESSED

Cauliflower is truly having its day in the spotlight! Riced, roasted, cut into steaks, made into a pizza crust: it is a versatile vegetable. This preparation is simple and filling and is elevated by the fresh salsa on top. The sumac adds a surprising twist to the salsa that takes this dish to the next level.

INGREDIENTS

CAULIFLOWER

2 heads cauliflower

¼ cup (60 ml) extra virgin olive oil

½ teaspoon garlic powder

½ teaspoon paprika

½ teaspoon sea salt

½ teaspoon freshly ground black pepper

Food Fact: Garlic is fat free, saturated fat free, cholesterol free, sodium free, and an immunity booster

SALSA

1 cup (150 g) cherry tomatoes, quartered

½ cup (90 g) seeded and diced roasted bell pepper

1 shallot, minced

1 clove garlic, minced

½ cup (15 g) fresh parsley leaves

½ cup (15 g) fresh basil leaves, torn

½ cup (15 g) fresh mint leaves, torn

½ cup (50 g) pitted kalamata olives, roughly chopped

¼ teaspoon sea salt

½ teaspoon freshly ground black pepper

½ teaspoon ground sumac

3 tablespoons (45 ml) freshly squeezed lemon juice

2 tablespoons (30 ml) extra virgin olive oil

METHOD OF PREPARATION

1. Preheat a grill to medium heat. Line a baking sheet with parchment paper.

2. To make the cauliflower, remove and discard the outer leaves from each head of cauliflower, and trim the stem so that it lies flat on the cutting board. Make sure to leave the core intact!

3. Cut the cauliflower into ¾-inch (2 cm) thick steaks. Reserve any loose florets for another time. Arrange in a single layer on the prepared baking sheet (you may need two baking sheets).

4. In a small bowl, whisk together the olive oil, garlic powder, paprika, salt, and pepper.

5. Brush the mixture evenly on to all the steaks.

6. Transfer to the grill and cook for 6 to 8 minutes on each side or until charred and tender.

7. Meanwhile, make the salsa. In a large bowl, combine all the salsa ingredients and toss to coat. Season to taste.

8. To serve, arrange the cauliflower steaks on a platter and top with the salsa. May be served hot or at room temperature.

COLD FARFALLE SALAD
WITH PESTO AND TOMATOES

SOY FREE, SUGAR FREE

INGREDIENTS

PESTO
¼ cup (10 g) nutritional yeast

2 cloves garlic peeled

⅓ cup (45 g) macadamia nuts

¼ cup (35 g) pine nuts, toasted

¾ teaspoon sea salt

½ teaspoon freshly ground black pepper

6 cups (240 g) fresh basil leaves

1 teaspoon freshly squeezed lemon juice

¾ cup (180 ml) extra virgin olive oil

PASTA SALAD
2 tablespoons (30 ml) olive oil

1 sweet onion, diced

4 cloves garlic, minced

2 pints (300 g) mixed heirloom
   grape tomatoes, halved

1 pound (455 g) farfalle, cooked according
   to package directions, drained

1 cup (240 ml) reserved pasta cooking liquid

1 cup (40 g) fresh basil leaves, torn

Food Fact: Grape tomatoes are low calorie, very low in fat, cholesterol free, sodium free, and a good source of fiber, lycopene, vitamins A and C

One of the things I get asked the most from my plant-based friends is to give them recipes that their non-plant-based friends will love, especially in the summer BBQ months. Most picnic and BBQ sides are laden with mayonnaise, cheese, bacon, etc. This pasta salad is creamy and hearty and pairs perfectly with whatever is being served at the picnic or BBQ. And even better, most people don't even question that it's plant-based—it's that good!

METHOD OF PREPARATION

1. To make the pesto, in the bowl of a food processor, combine the nutritional yeast, garlic, macadamia nuts, pine nuts, salt, and pepper. Pulse until chopped and combined.

2. Add the basil leaves and lemon juice and blend for 30 seconds, slowly drizzling in the olive oil, until combined. Set aside.

3. To make the pasta salad, in a large sauté pan over medium heat, add the oil and diced onion. Sauté for 3 to 5 minutes or until softened and lightly caramelized. Add the garlic and grape tomatoes. Stir for 1 minute.

4. In a large bowl, combine the cooked farfalle and pesto. Loosen the pesto with some of the reserved cooking liquid; you may not need all of it. Stir in the onion-tomato mixture and the torn basil leaves.

5. Serve at room temperature or cold.

JACKFRUIT JERK CARNITAS
WITH PINEAPPLE-MANGO SALSA

GRAIN FREE, NUT FREE

Jackfruit is an exotic tropical fruit that is part of the Moraceae family, which includes figs, mulberries, and breadfruit. It is a massive fruit that, when peeled, has a pulled meat-like texture. You can find it readily in grocery stores, either in the refrigerated section (typically already flavored) or canned in brine. Always rinse and drain it when it is brined. I also like to pick it over, as sometimes you will find hard round seeds left in the mix; just discard those.

INGREDIENTS

JACKFRUIT

Two 20-ounce (560 g) cans young jackfruit
in brine

1 tablespoon (15 ml) avocado oil

1 bunch green onions, finely chopped, green and
white parts divided

6 cloves garlic, minced

1 tablespoon (8 g) peeled and minced fresh ginger

1 habanero pepper, minced (less for less spice)

3 tablespoons (24 g) Jamaican jerk seasoning

2 tablespoons (30 ml) freshly squeezed lime juice

1 tablespoon (15 g) tomato paste

2 tablespoons (25 g) coconut sugar

3 tablespoons (45 ml) tamari

SALSA

1 cup (175 g) peeled, pitted, and diced mango

1 cup (175 g) diced pineapple

½ cup (60 g) seeded and diced red bell pepper

¼ cup (40 g) diced red onion

1 jalapeño pepper, seeded and diced

¼ cup (5 g) finely chopped fresh cilantro

2 tablespoons (30 ml) freshly squeezed lime juice

½ teaspoon sea salt

FOR SERVING

8 corn tortillas, warmed

1 avocado, peeled, pitted, and thinly sliced

½ cup (60 g) shredded lettuce

Food Fact: Jackfruit is fat free, saturated fat free, cholesterol free, sodium free, excellent source of vitamin C, and a good source of fiber, vitamin B2, copper, manganese, magnesium, and potassium

METHOD OF PREPARATION

1. To make the jackfruit, rinse and drain it really well. Pick through it and remove all of the seedpods and tough parts. You want to keep the shredded meat-like pieces. Chop any large pieces. Place all the jackfruit shreds in a clean dish towel and squeeze to remove any excess liquid. Set aside.

2. In a large sauté pan over medium heat, add the oil and heat until hot. Add the white parts of the green onions, garlic, ginger, and habanero. Cook, stirring frequently, for 5 minutes.

3. Add the jackfruit and continue to cook for 6 minutes or until the jackfruit is completely dry and caramelized.

4. Add the jerk seasoning and stir for 1 minute.

5. Add the lime juice, tomato paste, coconut sugar, and tamari, and cook, stirring occasionally, for 12 to 15 minutes or until all the liquid has been cooked off. Salt and pepper to taste.

6. Meanwhile, make the salsa. In a large bowl, combine all the salsa ingredients and toss to coat. Allow to sit and let the flavors develop while the carnitas continue to cook.

7. To assemble, top the warmed corn tortilla with shredded lettuce, a large scoop of jackfruit carnitas, top with the salsa, and add a few avocado slices.

CHICKPEA SALAD SANDWICHES
WITH QUICK PICKLES

GRAIN FREE, NUT FREE, SOY FREE

The trick to this salad is to really dry the chickpeas. I like to lay them out on a kitchen towel to really ensure they all get dry. This perfect sandwich is ideal to take on a picnic. Serve it alongside a pasta salad or simple green salad for a delicious lunch. Make sure you save the liquid from the chickpeas! It's called aquafaba and we use it throughout this book as an egg replacer.

INGREDIENTS

QUICK PICKLES

1 cup (240 ml) water

⅓ cup (80 ml) apple cider vinegar

2 tablespoons (25 g) raw unprocessed cane sugar

1 teaspoon sea salt

2 cups (240 g) thinly sliced Kirby cucumbers

½ cup (60 g) thinly sliced sweet onion

Food Fact: Cucumbers are fat free, saturated fat free, sodium free, cholesterol free, low calorie, and a good source of vitamin C

CHICKPEA SALAD

One 14-ounce (392 g) can chickpeas, drained and rinsed

2 tablespoons (30 ml) freshly squeezed lemon juice

3 tablespoons (45 g) hummus

2 teaspoons Dijon mustard

½ cup (55 g) diced celery

½ cup (60 g) diced red onion

2 tablespoons (20 g) sweet pickle relish

¼ teaspoon sea salt

¼ teaspoon freshly ground black pepper

¼ teaspoon celery seed

¼ teaspoon paprika

FOR SERVING

8 slices great-quality artisan bread

1 cup (30 g) mixed baby greens

1 cup (50 g) sprouts

METHOD OF PREPARATION

1. To make the quick pickles, combine the water, vinegar, sugar, and salt in a medium bowl. Stir until the sugar and salt dissolve. Add the cucumbers and sweet onion and toss to coat. Allow to sit while you make your sandwich. These may be stored in an airtight container in the refrigerator for up to a week.

2. To make the chickpea salad, make sure the chickpeas are very dry and then add them to the bowl of a food processor. Pulse 10 to 15 times or until roughly chopped; do not over process.

3. Scrape the chunky chickpeas into a large bowl and add the lemon juice, hummus, Dijon, celery, red onion, relish, salt, pepper, celery seed, and paprika. Stir to combine.

4. To assemble the sandwiches, toast the bread if you prefer, top with a large scoop of the salad, the mixed baby greens, and the sprouts, then top with the remaining bread. Serve with the quick pickles.

PERFECT PICNIC CRISPY PURPLE POTATO SALAD

SERVES 8

GLUTEN FREE, GRAIN FREE, NUT FREE, SOY FREE, SUGAR FREE

INGREDIENTS

2 pounds (910 g) new purple potatoes, quartered into 1-inch (2.5 cm) pieces

2 tablespoons (30 ml) avocado oil

1 teaspoon sea salt

1 teaspoon paprika

½ teaspoon freshly ground black pepper

2 shallots, thinly sliced

⅓ cup (80 ml) apple cider vinegar

3 tablespoons (33 g) Dijon mustard

3 tablespoons (12 g) chopped fresh parsley

½ cup (120 ml) extra virgin olive oil

You will not believe how beautiful and simple this potato salad is. The purple potatoes can easily be replaced with a red new potato if you are having difficulty finding the purple ones. This salad is wonderful warm or at room temperature as the perfect picnic accompaniment.

METHOD OF PREPARATION

1. Preheat the oven to 400°F (200°C). Line a baking sheet with parchment; set aside.

2. In a large bowl, combine the potatoes, avocado oil, salt, paprika, and pepper. Toss to evenly coat. Spread in a single layer on the prepared baking sheet.

3. Transfer to the oven and roast until tender and golden brown, 25 to 30 minutes. Let cool for 15 minutes.

4. In a large bowl, combine the shallots, vinegar, Dijon, and parsley. Whisk to combine and then slowly drizzle in the olive oil, whisking until incorporated.

5. When the potatoes are partially cool, toss them into the vinaigrette. Serve warm or at room temperature.

PORTOBELLO AND PEPPER FAJITAS WITH GUACAMOLE

GLUTEN FREE, GRAIN FREE, NUT FREE, SOY FREE, SUGAR FREE, UNPROCESSED

Fajitas are a quick and delectable dinner that showcase fresh vegetables. The colors in these fajitas are just so beautiful, you are truly eating the rainbow! They come together quickly, so make sure you have all of your chopping done ahead of time to have dinner ready in minutes.

INGREDIENTS

GUACAMOLE

2 avocados, peeled and pitted

Juice of 1 lime

¼ cup (40 g) minced red onion

¼ teaspoon sea salt

FAJITAS

2 tablespoons (30 ml) avocado or coconut oil, divided

1 poblano pepper, seeded and thinly sliced

1 yellow bell pepper, seeded and thinly sliced

1 red bell pepper, seeded and thinly sliced

1 jalapeño, seeded and thinly sliced

1 sweet onion, halved and thinly sliced

3 large portobello mushrooms, wiped, stems removed, gills scraped clean, and thinly sliced

2 teaspoons red wine vinegar

1 teaspoon chili powder

¾ teaspoon ground cumin

½ teaspoon dried oregano

½ teaspoon onion powder

½ teaspoon garlic powder

½ teaspoon paprika

½ teaspoon sea salt

¼ teaspoon freshly ground black pepper

FOR SERVING

8 corn or flour tortillas

¼ cup (5 g) cilantro leaves

¼ cup (40 g) salsa (optional)

Food Fact: Bell peppers are fat free, saturated fat free, low sodium, cholesterol free, low calorie, and high in vitamin C

METHOD OF PREPARATION

1. To make the guacamole. In a medium bowl, combine the avocado flesh, lime juice, red onion, and salt. Mash to combine. Set aside.

2. To make the fajitas, heat a large skillet or flat top over high heat. Add 1 tablespoon (15 ml) of the oil and, once hot, add the poblano, yellow and red bell peppers, jalapeño, and onion. Cook until softened and lightly caramelized, stirring frequently, 2 to 3 minutes. Transfer to a large bowl and keep warm.

3. Add the remaining 1 tablespoon (15 ml) oil to the pan and, once hot, add the mushrooms, vinegar, chili powder, cumin, oregano, onion powder, garlic powder, paprika, salt, and pepper. Cook, stirring frequently, for 2 to 3 minutes or until tender and lightly caramelized. Add the peppers back to the pan and stir to coat in the seasoning.

4. While the vegetables are cooking, warm the tortillas and keep warm in the oven in aluminum foil.

5. To serve, spoon the fajita mixture into the warmed tortilla and top with the guacamole, cilantro, and salsa if desired.

MUSHROOM BBQ SANDWICHES WITH RED CABBAGE SLAW

SERVES 4

GRAIN FREE, NUT FREE, SOY FREE

This recipe is a little time-consuming, but so worth it! If you are a little tight on time, you can substitute your favorite BBQ sauce for the homemade one. The extra step of roasting the shredded mushrooms prior to sautéing in the sauce gives a depth of textures that truly makes this sandwich exceptional… well, that plus the crunch and tang of the slaw and pickles!

INGREDIENTS

BBQ SAUCE

1½ cups (360 ml) organic no-sugar-added ketchup

¼ cup (50 g) coconut sugar

2 tablespoons (30 ml) molasses

2 cloves garlic, minced

¼ cup (60 ml) apple cider vinegar

2 tablespoons (30 ml) vegan Worcestershire sauce

2 teaspoons sweet paprika

1 teaspoon freshly ground black pepper

1 teaspoon dry mustard

½ teaspoon favorite hot sauce

MUSHROOMS

6 king oyster or royal trumpet mushrooms

3 tablespoons (45 ml) avocado oil

2 teaspoons smoked paprika

½ teaspoon sea salt

¼ teaspoon cayenne pepper

3 cloves garlic, minced

SLAW

1 small head cabbage, shredded

¼ cup (40 g) thinly sliced red onion

1 jalapeño, seeded and thinly sliced

½ cup (120 ml) apple cider vinegar

¼ cup (50 g) raw cane sugar

¾ teaspoon sea salt

1 teaspoon celery seed

FOR SERVING

A couple slices of favorite sliced pickles

4 favorite hamburger buns

Food Fact: Mushrooms are fat free, saturated fat free, very low sodium, cholesterol free, low calorie, high in vitamin B2, and a good source of vitamins B3, B5, and copper

METHOD OF PREPARATION

1. To make the BBQ sauce, in a large, heavy-bottomed pan, combine the ketchup, sugar, molasses, garlic, vinegar, Worcestershire, paprika, black pepper, mustard, and hot sauce. Simmer over medium-low heat for 15 to 20 minutes or until the sauce has deepened in color.

2. Preheat the oven to 400°F (200°C). Line a baking sheet with parchment paper; set aside.

3. Meanwhile, make the mushrooms. Slice mushrooms thinly from the top of the cap and transfer them to the prepared baking sheet. Drizzle the mushrooms with the avocado oil, paprika, salt, cayenne, and garlic. Toss to evenly coat.

4. Transfer to the oven and bake for 20 minutes or until the mushrooms are browned and crispy on the edges.

5. While the mushrooms are cooking, make the slaw. In a large bowl, combine the shredded cabbage, red onion, jalapeño, vinegar, sugar, salt, and celery seed. Toss to coat and allow to marinate while the rest of the dish comes together.

6. Once the mushrooms have cooked, transfer them to a large sauté pan along with 1 cup (240 ml) of the BBQ sauce. Toss to coat. The remainder of the sauce can be stored in an airtight container in the refrigerator for up to 3 weeks.

7. To assemble, scoop the mushrooms onto the buns and top with the pickles and slaw.

VEGAN BEET AND MUSHROOM BURGER

SERVES 6

NUT FREE, SUGAR FREE

This burger is just scrumptious! It's made with tempeh, a soybean product. Unlike tofu, tempeh is made using whole fermented soybeans which gives it a higher protein, fiber, and vitamin content than the more processed tofu. Tempeh, sautéed mushrooms, brown rice, and beets come together to create the patty. What puts this burger over the top are really the 'buttered' onions, pickles, and pretzel bun. Hearty and filling, this burger will definitely become one of your Summer favorites.

INGREDIENTS

BURGER

1 tablespoon avocado oil

1½ cups cremini mushrooms, cleaned and sliced

1 cup cooked short grain brown rice, cooled

8 ounces tempeh, chopped

2 tablespoons beets, grated

¼ cup quick cooking oats

1 teaspoon kosher salt

1 teaspoon freshly ground black pepper

1 tablespoon nutritional yeast

1 teaspoon garlic powder

1 teaspoon onion powder

ONIONS

3 tablespoons vegan butter, such as miyokos

2 cups sweet onion, diced

6 pretzel slider buns or buns of your choice

TOPPINGS (OPTIONAL)

6 sliced vegan cheddar cheese

Sliced pickles

6 pieces butter lettuce

6 slices tomato

METHOD OF PREPARATION

1. Add the avocado oil to a large sauté pan over medium heat. Once hot, add the sliced mushrooms and sauté until tender and browned, about 8 to 10 minutes.

2. In the bowl of a food processor, combine the cooked mushrooms, cooked rice, chopped tempeh, beets, oats, salt, pepper, nutritional yeast, garlic powder, and onion powder. Pulse until the mixture resembles ground hamburger.

3. Divide the mixture into 6 equal rounds. I like to wet my hands to help form them into patties. Place on a plate and into the refrigerator for 30 minutes. While the burgers are resting, make the onions.

4. On a griddle, melt the butter over medium high heat. Once melted, add in the diced onions and sauté for 10 to 12 minutes, stirring occasionally, until tender and golden brown. Remove from the griddle leaving behind as much butter as you can.

5. Remove the burgers from the refrigerator and transfer them one by one to the hot griddle. Cook for 3 minutes one each side, allowing a crust to form and then turn over. If you wish to have cheese on your burgers, place it on top of the burger while the second side cooks and allow the cheese to melt.

6. Lightly toast buns while the burgers are cooking.

7. To assemble, place a burger on the bottom of a lightly toasted bun, top with caramelized onions, the pickles, lettuce, tomato, and the top of the bun. Enjoy immediately.

WHITE PEACH AND FIG GRANITA

GLUTEN FREE, GRAIN FREE, NUT FREE, RAW, SOY FREE, UNPROCESSED

INGREDIENTS

2 cups (480 ml) water

½ cup (100 g) coconut sugar

5 ripe white peaches, pitted and chopped

5 fresh ripe figs, chopped

Food Fact: Figs are fat free, cholesterol free, sodium free, and a good source of dietary fiber and potassium

This is seriously one of the simplest desserts possible, but when made with perfectly ripened summer peaches and figs, the flavor is otherwordly! Do not even try to make this any other time of year, or you will be disappointed by the lack of flavor. This takes a little bit of time but can easily be made ahead for a perfectly elegant summer dessert.

METHOD OF PREPARATION

1. In a medium saucepan over medium heat, combine the water and sugar and stir until the sugar is dissolved, about 5 minutes; allow to cool.

2. In the bowl of a food processor, add the peaches and figs and process until smooth.

3. Add the pureed fruit to the sugar mixture and stir to combine.

4. Pour the mixture into an 8 x 8-inch (20 x 20 cm) metal baking dish and place in the freezer for 1 hour.

5. After 1 hour, remove the baking dish from the freezer and, using a fork, rake the top of the granita. Transfer back to the freezer and freeze for 1 hour more. Repeat every hour for 4 hours or until the mixture has a snow-like texture.

PEACH CRUMBLE

GLUTEN FREE, GRAIN FREE, SOY FREE

INGREDIENTS

8 ripe peaches, pitted and sliced

1 tablespoon (15 ml) bourbon
   whiskey (optional)

1 teaspoon vanilla extract

Juice of 1 lemon

2 tablespoons (30 ml) maple syrup

1 cup (80 g) old-fashioned rolled oats

½ cup (60 g) almond meal

½ cup (70 g) pecans, chopped

¼ cup (50 g) coconut sugar

½ teaspoon ground cinnamon

¼ teaspoon sea salt

½ cup (120 ml) coconut oil, at
   room temperature

Food Fact: Peaches are low fat,
saturated fat free, sodium free,
cholesterol free, and a good
source of vitamin C

A crumble takes me back to childhood summer
days when peaches were falling off the trees
begging to be eaten in every way possible. This
one served warm with some almond or cashew
vanilla ice cream can transport you back to those
endless summer nights where anything seemed
possible. The bourbon is optional, but it gives this
a depth of flavor that is exceptional.

METHOD OF PREPARATION

1. Preheat the oven to 350°F (180°C).

2. In a large bowl, combine the sliced
peaches with the whiskey (if using), vanilla,
lemon juice, and maple syrup. Toss to evenly
coat. Transfer to an 8 x 8-inch (20 x 20 cm)
baking dish.

3. In a large bowl, combine the oats, almond
meal, pecans, coconut sugar, cinnamon, and
salt. Add the coconut oil and, using your
hands, mix until evenly distributed and the
mixture has a sandy texture.

4. Top the peaches with the crumb mixture.

5. Transfer to the oven and bake for 25 to
30 minutes or until browned and bubbly.
Allow to cool for 5 minutes before serving.

DARK CHERRY CLAFOUTIS

SERVES 8

INGREDIENTS

One 12-ounce (340 g) package silken tofu

½ cup (60 g) almond flour

½ cup (120 ml) maple syrup

½ cup (120 g) applesauce

1 tablespoon (8 g) tapioca flour

1 tablespoon (15 ml) coconut oil,
    at room temperature, plus more for greasing

1 teaspoon vanilla extract

1 teaspoon almond extract

¼ teaspoon sea salt

¾ cup (120 g) pitted dark cherries

Organic powdered sugar, for dusting (optional)

Food Fact: Cherries are fat free, saturated fat free, sodium free, cholesterol free, and a good source of vitamin C and potassium

Clafoutis is a baked French dessert that is traditionally made with a flan-like batter of eggs and milk. This one trades those in for silken tofu, which creates a creamy texture that is both light and decadent at the same time. The summer dark cherries add a color and flavor like no other. I love to serve this warm dusted with a little powdered sugar.

METHOD OF PREPARATION

1. Preheat the oven to 350°F (180°C). Grease a pie dish with a little coconut oil and set aside.

2. In a high-speed blender, combine the tofu, almond flour, maple syrup, applesauce, tapioca flour, coconut oil, vanilla, almond extract, and salt. Puree on high speed until smooth and creamy, about 1 minute.

3. Pour into the prepared pie dish. Arrange the cherries on top.

4. Transfer to the oven and bake for 45 to 50 minutes or until lightly browned and set.

5. Serve hot or cold, dusted with powdered sugar, if desired.

TWO-INGREDIENT CANTALOUPE ICE CREAM

SERVES 8

GLUTEN FREE, GRAIN FREE, RAW, SOY FREE, SUGAR FREE, UNPROCESSED

INGREDIENTS

1 cantaloupe melon, peeled, seeded, and cut into 1-inch (2.5 cm) pieces (about 4 cups [560 g])

4 medium bananas, peeled and cut into 1-inch (2.5 cm) pieces

Food Fact: Cantaloupe is fat free, saturated fat free, very low sodium, cholesterol free, high in vitamins A and C, and a good source of folate

The summer melon, so sweet and juicy, really is a perfect food when eaten in season. This ice cream could not be simpler or more refreshing. You could make this with honeydew, Galia, muskmelon, or Crenshaw melon as well.

METHOD OF PREPARATION

1. Place the cantaloupe and banana pieces on a baking sheet that will fit in your freezer. Transfer the baking sheet to the freezer and allow to freeze overnight.

2. Place all the frozen fruit into a high-speed blender or food processor. Pulse until completely smooth and creamy.

3. Transfer to a freezer-safe container or serve immediately!

DARK CHOCOLATE-COVERED
WATERMELON BITES WITH SEA SALT

SERVES 6

GLUTEN FREE, GRAIN FREE, NUT FREE, SOY FREE

INGREDIENTS

3 cups (450 g) cubed seedless watermelon
   in 1-inch (2.5 cm) pieces

Mini skewers or toothpicks

1 cup (175 g) chopped dairy-free
   dark chocolate

2 tablespoons (30 ml) coconut oil

Maldon sea salt

OPTIONAL
Slivered almonds

Coconut flakes

Food Fact: Watermelon is fat free, saturated fat free, sodium free, cholesterol free, high in vitamins A and C, and a great source of lycopene

Watermelon is a summer staple, and this recipe kicks it up a notch. Dark chocolate, watermelon, and sea salt come together for the perfect summer treat. I love to take these to the beach, on a picnic, or to a BBQ for a refreshing and healthy dessert or snack.

METHOD OF PREPARATION

1. Line a large baking sheet with parchment paper or wax paper. Arrange the watermelon cubes on the paper so that they are not touching. Place a toothpick or small skewer in each cube of watermelon and transfer to the freezer for 30 minutes.

2. While the watermelon is freezing, melt the chocolate in a double boiler or microwave at 30-second intervals. Stir in the coconut oil.

3. Dip the frozen cubes of watermelon into the melted chocolate, sprinkle with the salt, and return to the parchment paper to set. You can also dress them up with slivered almonds and coconut flakes.

4. Serve immediately or store in the freezer until ready to serve.

WATERMELON VODKA LEMONADE SLUSHIE

SERVES 6

GLUTEN FREE, GRAIN FREE, NUT FREE, RAW, SOY FREE

INGREDIENTS

4 cups (600 g) cubed seedless watermelon

2 cups (480 ml) good-quality lemonade

10 ounces (280 ml) vodka, chilled

2 cups (300 g) crushed ice

This is for those lazy summer afternoons when a refreshing adult beverage is needed. You could easily make these sans alcohol as well, just substitute the vodka for more lemonade and blend to perfection. I love to serve these in a frozen glass for even more chilled deliciousness.

METHOD OF PREPARATION

1. Place all the ingredients in a high-powered blender and blend until smooth.

2. Serve immediately.

FROZEN ORANGE DREAMSICLE PIE

GLUTEN FREE, GRAIN FREE, SOY FREE

Who doesn't love the sound of the ice cream truck coming down the street during summer? I sure did! And the dreamsicle was one of my favorite orders. This pie recreates that flavor in a healthier way. The crust is chewy and slightly sweet, the middle is fresh orange-flavored heaven, and the top, well we know how I love some dreamy whipped coconut cream! This will become a summer favorite for kids and adults alike.

INGREDIENTS

CRUST

1 cup (140 g) raw almonds

½ cup (70 g) pecans

3 Medjool dates, pitted

¼ teaspoon sea salt

FILLING

2 cups (280 g) raw cashews, soaked for at least 4 hours, drained, and rinsed

⅓ cup (80 ml) maple syrup

½ cup (120 ml) coconut oil

3 tablespoons (18 g) freshly grated orange zest

⅓ cup (80 ml) freshly squeezed orange juice

1½ teaspoons vanilla extract

WHIPPED COCONUT CREAM

One 14-ounce (392 g) can full-fat coconut milk, refrigerated overnight

1 tablespoon (15 ml) vanilla extract

2 teaspoons maple syrup

METHOD OF PREPARATION

1. Line a 7-inch (18 cm) springform pan with parchment paper.

2. To make the crust, add the almonds, pecans, dates, and sea salt to the bowl of a food processor. Process until a sticky dough forms. Add a splash of water if needed to bring it all together.

3. Press the crust into the prepared pan, making sure you bring it about 1 inch (2.5 cm) up the sides of the pan.

4. To make the filling, add the soaked and rinsed cashews, maple syrup, coconut oil orange zest, orange juice, and vanilla to a high-speed blender. Blend until smooth and creamy.

5. Pour into the springform pan and smooth with a spatula.

6. Cover and transfer to the freezer for at least 3 hours.

7. While the pie is freezing, make the whipped cream. Start by placing your mixing bowl in the freezer for 10 minutes.

8. Once your bowl is cold, remove the can of cold coconut milk from the refrigerator. Carefully remove the top of the can; do not shake or tip upside down. Scoop the thick layer of coconut cream from the top of the can, leaving the water at the bottom for another use.

9. Using a whisk attachment, beat the coconut cream on medium speed for 2 to 4 minutes, or until the cream becomes light and fluffy and peaks form. Add the vanilla and maple syrup and beat until just incorporated.

10. When ready to serve, pipe of dollop the whipped cream onto the pie and enjoy!

CHOCOLATE CHIP COOKIE ICE CREAM SANDWICHES

SERVES 8

GRAIN FREE, SOY FREE

INGREDIENTS

½ cup (120 g) vegan butter, such as Miyoko's, or coconut oil

1¼ cups (250 g) coconut brown sugar

2 teaspoons vanilla extract

¼ cup (60 ml) unsweetened almond milk

¼ cup (60 g) unsweetened applesauce

2¼ cups (270 g) unbleached all-purpose flour

1 teaspoon baking soda

½ teaspoon sea salt

2 cups (340 g) dairy-free dark chocolate chips

2 pints (480 g each) good-quality almond or coconut vanilla bean ice cream, softened

The ice cream sandwich is synonymous with summer for so many of us. These cookies are chewy and crispy all at the same time. Combined with your favorite dairy-free ice cream, they are an easy and delightful dessert for any summer night.

METHOD OF PREPARATION

1. Preheat the oven to 375°F (190°C). Line two baking sheets with parchment paper; set aside.

2. In a large bowl using a handheld mixer, beat the butter and sugar on medium speed until light and fluffy. Beat in the vanilla, milk, and applesauce and blend for 2 more minutes or until combined.

3. In a separate large bowl, whisk together the flour, baking soda, and salt.

4. Add the dry ingredients to the wet using a wooden spoon to stir until incorporated. Fold in the chocolate chips.

5. Using a cookie scoop, scoop the dough onto the prepared baking sheets.

6. Transfer to the oven and bake for 9 to 11 minutes or until golden brown and chewy in the center. Allow to cool for 15 minutes and then transfer to a wire rack to cool completely.

7. While the cookies are cooling, scoop the softened ice cream into balls and place on a baking sheet or large plate. Transfer to the freezer and freeze until ready to use.

8. Once the cookies have cooled completely, remove the frozen ice cream from the freezer, sandwich in between two cookies, and serve!

BLACKBERRY AND BRANDY-SOAKED POUND CAKE PARFAITS

GRAIN FREE, SOY FREE

Pound cake, blackberries, and parfait... need I say more? These treats are so appealing to the eye and the stomach. They are sweet, tart, crunchy, and soft and make the perfect addition to any summer event. Do not skip the step of the parchment overhang for the pound cake. It makes removal from the pan simple and effortless.

INGREDIENTS

POUND CAKE
Coconut oil spray

½ cup (120 g) vegan butter, such as Miyoko's

1 cup (200 g) raw cane sugar

2 teaspoons vanilla extract

2 cups (240 g) unbleached all-purpose flour

1 tablespoon (8 g) baking powder

½ teaspoon sea salt

1 cup (240 ml) unsweetened almond milk

1 tablespoon (15 ml) apple cider vinegar

BLACKBERRY MASH
2 pints (250 g each) fresh blackberries

½ cup (120 g) blackberry jam

¼ cup (60 ml) hot water

2 tablespoons (30 ml) brandy (optional)

OPTIONAL (FOR SERVING)
½ cup (60 g) sliced almonds, toasted

METHOD OF PREPARATION

1. Preheat the oven to 350°F (180°C). Grease a 9 x 5-inch (23 x 13 cm) loaf pan with coconut oil spray, and line with parchment paper that hangs over the sides. Set aside.

2. To make the pound cake, in the bowl of an electric mixer or with a handheld mixer, beat the butter and sugar on medium speed for 2 minutes or until light and fluffy. Add the vanilla and beat for 1 minute longer.

3. In another large bowl, sift together the flour, baking powder, and salt. Add to the butter mixture, beating on medium for 2 minutes or until combined.

4. To make your vegan buttermilk, in a small bowl, combine the milk with the apple cider vinegar, stirring until it curdles.

5. Add the buttermilk to the other ingredients and stir with a wooden spoon until combined, about 1 minute. The batter will be thick. Do not overmix.

6. Pour the batter into the prepared loaf pan and transfer to the oven. Bake for 50 to 60 minutes, or until a toothpick inserted in the center comes out clean.

7. Lift the cake out of the pan using the parchment paper overhang and allow to cool completely before making the parfaits.

8. To make the blackberry mash, add the blackberries to a large bowl. With a potato masher, lightly smash them until they are loose and juicy. Add the jam, hot water, and brandy (if using). Mix to combine. Set aside to cool.

9. When ready to assemble the parfaits, have 6 small mason jars or glass juice glasses at the ready.

10. Cut the pound cake into 18 uniform pieces, 3 per jar. Add one piece to the bottom of the jar, spoon some blackberry mash on top, and repeat with another slice of cake, more mash, more cake, and more mash. Then sprinkle the last layer with the sliced toasted almonds.

11. Eat immediately or allow the blackberry mash to get all soaked up in the pound cake.

FALL RECIPES

FRUITS & VEGETABLES IN SEASON

Acorn Squash • Asian Pear • Black Salsify • Broccoli

Brussels Sprouts • Butter Lettuce • Butternut Squash • Cactus Pear

Cauliflower • Chayote Squash • Chinese Long Beans • Crab Apples

Cranberries • Date Plum • Delicata Squash • Daikon Radish • Garlic

Ginger • Grapes • Guava • Hearts of Palm • Jalapeño Peppers

Jerusalem Artichokes • Key Limes • Kohlrabi • Kumquats

Muscadine Grapes • Mushrooms • Passion Fruit • Pears • Persimmons

Pineapple • Pomegranate • Pumpkin • Quince • Radicchio

Sweet Potatoes • Swiss Chard • Turnips

COCONUT CURRY LAKSA

GLUTEN FREE, SOY FREE

Laksa is a spicy noodle soup with a base of curried coconut milk. This one does not disappoint. The complexity of the homemade curry paste is well worth the time and effort. The fall vegetables and noodles make this a hearty, one-dish meal.

INGREDIENTS

CURRY PASTE

2 teaspoons coriander seeds

½ teaspoon cumin seeds

½ teaspoon fennel seeds

1-inch (2.5 cm) piece turmeric root, peeled

1-inch (2.5 cm) piece fresh ginger, peeled

1 green chile

½ teaspoon cayenne pepper

1 stalk lemongrass, smashed and roughly chopped

4 cloves garlic, peeled

2 tablespoons (18 g) raw cashews, soaked for 30 minutes, rinsed, and drained

½ cup (8 g) cilantro leaves

2 teaspoons freshly squeezed lime juice

Food Fact: Swiss chard is fat free, cholesterol free, a good source of magnesium, and an excellent source of vitamins A and C

SOUP

1 tablespoon (15 ml) coconut oil

2 cups (140 g) sliced brown mushrooms

1 cup (120 g) peeled and thinly sliced carrot

½ cup (60 g) thinly sliced and seeded red bell pepper

½ cup (35 g) broccoli florets

3 cups (720 ml) vegetable broth

One 14-ounce (392 g) can full-fat coconut milk

8 ounces (225 g) dried brown rice noodles

1 cup (30 g) roughly chopped Swiss chard

1 tablespoon (12 g) coconut sugar (optional)

FOR SERVING

¼ cup (80 g) pomegranate arils

¼ cup (4 g) cilantro leaves, chopped

¼ cup (15 g) mint leaves, chopped

1 lime, quartered

METHOD OF PREPARATION

1. To make the curry paste, in a small sauté pan over medium heat, toast the coriander, cumin, and fennel seeds until fragrant, about 2 minutes, tossing so as not to burn. Add to a spice grinder and grind to a coarse texture.

2. Add the toasted spices, turmeric root, ginger, chile, cayenne, lemongrass, garlic, cashews, cilantro, and lime juice to the bowl of a food processor. Blend until a paste forms, about 1 minute. Reserve.

3. To make the soup, in a large stockpot over medium heat, add the coconut oil. Once hot, add all of the the curry paste and stir-fry for 3 minutes.

4. Add the mushrooms to the pan and cook, stirring frequently, for another 2 minutes.

5. Add the carrots, bell pepper, broccoli, broth, and coconut milk. Increase the heat to high and bring to a boil. Reduce the heat to medium-low, add the rice noodles, and simmer for 10 minutes.

6. Add the Swiss chard and stir to wilt. Taste and adjust the seasonings, adding the coconut sugar if desired.

7. To serve, ladle into bowls and serve with the pomegranate arils, cilantro, mint, and lime wedges.

TUSCAN KALE CAESAR SALAD WITH CRISPY CHICKPEAS

GRAIN FREE

Caesar salad is such a wonderful addition to so many meals, not to mention a delightful lunch on it's own. This one is hearty and light at the same time. The croutons have been replaced by crispy roasted chickpeas and the romaine replaced by nutritious Tuscan kale. Make sure you massage the dressing into the kale, allowing the tough cell structure to break down and be more palatable.

INGREDIENTS

DRESSING

1 tablespoon (11 g) Dijon mustard

2 tablespoons (5 g) nutritional yeast

½ cup (120 g) avocado oil mayonnaise

2 cloves garlic, crushed

2 teaspoons capers, drained

2 tablespoons (30 ml) freshly squeezed
    lemon juice

1 tablespoon (15 ml) tamari

1 tablespoon (15 ml) maple syrup

1 tablespoon (15 ml) extra virgin olive oil

1 teaspoon freshly ground black pepper

¼ teaspoon sea salt

CRISPY CHICKPEAS

One 15-ounce (420 g) can chickpeas,
    drained and rinsed

1 teaspoon garlic powder

1 tablespoon (15 ml) avocado oil

½ teaspoon sea salt

CASHEW PARMESAN

1 cup (140 g) raw cashews

¼ cup (10 g) nutritional yeast

1 teaspoon sea salt

1 teaspoon garlic powder

SALAD

3 bunches Tuscan kale, ribs removed and leaves
    shredded or chopped

METHOD OF PREPARATION

1. First make the dressing so the flavors have some time to meld together. In a high-powered blender, combine all the dressing ingredients. Blend on high speed until thick and creamy. Reserve.

2. Preheat the oven to 400°F (200°C). Line a baking sheet with parchment paper and set aside.

3. To make the chickpeas, in a medium bowl, add the drained chickpeas, garlic powder, avocado oil, and salt. Toss to combine and spread on the prepared baking sheet. Transfer to the oven and roast for 7 to 10 minutes or until lightly browned and crispy. Allow to cool while you make the cashew parmesan.

4. To make the cashew parmesan, combine the cashews, nutritional yeast, salt, and garlic powder in the bowl of a food processor. Pulse until chopped and resembling grated parmesan.

5. In a large bowl, add the shredded kale and the dressing. Using hands, massage the dressing into the kale. This infuses the kale with the dressing and allows it to break down the tough cell structure. The kale will reduce by about half in volume.

6. Transfer the dressed kale to a serving bowl, top with the crispy chickpeas and cashew parmesan, and serve.

BOMBAY BURRITO WITH CILANTRO CHUTNEY AND PICKLED ONIONS

SERVES 4

GRAIN FREE, SOY FREE

Yes, this burrito has many steps, and yes, it is well worth the effort. I love to whip up a batch of this filling on the weekend and make the burritos throughout the week, as I crave it again and again. The pickled onions and the chutney will each keep for about 1 week in an airtight container in the refrigerator. Try to find great-quality flaky tortillas; they are part of the shine in this incredibly tasty dish.

INGREDIENTS

PICKLED ONIONS

2 cups (320 g) thinly sliced red onion

1 cup (240 ml) red wine vinegar

¼ cup (50 g) raw cane sugar

1 teaspoon sea salt

1 teaspoon whole coriander seeds

1 teaspoon whole cumin seeds

1 teaspoon whole black peppercorns

CILANTRO CHUTNEY

½ cup (120 g) almond or cashew yogurt

¼ cup (60 ml) freshly squeezed lemon juice

1 bunch cilantro, leaves and tender stems

1 cup (48 g) mint leaves

1 jalapeño, roughly chopped

2 teaspoons freshly grated ginger

1 clove garlic

½ teaspoon sea salt

½ teaspoon raw cane sugar

1 tablespoon (15 ml) water

CURRIED POTATOES

2 cups (280 g) peeled and roughly chopped russet potatoes

2 cloves garlic, minced

1 tablespoon (15 ml) coconut oil

1 teaspoon sea salt

2 tablespoons (16 g) curry powder

ROASTED VEGETABLE FILLING

3 cups (300 g) cauliflower florets

One 14-ounce (392 g) can chickpeas, rinsed and drained well

2 tablespoons (30 ml) avocado oil

1 teaspoon sea salt

1 tablespoon (8 g) ground coriander

1 tablespoon (8 g) ground cumin

½ teaspoon crushed red pepper flakes

1 teaspoon whole coriander seeds

1 teaspoon whole fennel seeds

2 cups (60 g) baby spinach

BURRITO ASSEMBLY

4 large tortillas

METHOD OF PREPARATION

1. To make the pickled onions, combine the red onion, vinegar, sugar, salt, coriander, cumin, and peppercorns in a medium saucepan over medium-high heat. Bring to a boil, decrease the heat to low, and simmer for 2 minutes. Remove from the heat. These can be made up to 1 week ahead of time and stored in an airtight container in the fridge.

2. To make the cilantro chutney, combine the yogurt, lemon juice, cilantro, mint, jalapeño, ginger, garlic, salt, sugar, and water in a high-powered blender. Blend until smooth and creamy. This can be made up to 1 week ahead of time and stored in an airtight container in the fridge.

3. Preheat the oven to 425°F (220°C). Line a baking sheet with parchment paper and set aside.

4. To make the potatoes, in a large pot, add the potatoes and cover them with water. Bring to a boil over high heat, decrease the heat to medium, and cook until tender, 15 to 20 minutes.

5. While the potatoes are cooking, make the filling. Spread the cauliflower and chickpeas in a single layer on the prepared baking sheet. Drizzle with the avocado oil. Season with the salt, ground coriander, cumin, red pepper flakes, coriander seeds, and fennel seeds. Transfer to the oven and roast for 20 minutes or until the cauliflower is tender and browned, stirring halfway through the cooking.

6. Once the potatoes are tender, drain the water and reserve 1 cup (240 ml). Add them back to the pan along with the water, garlic, coconut oil, salt, and curry powder. Mash until combined and slightly chunky.

7. When ready to assemble, lay the tortillas out on a flat surface. Smear one-fourth of the potato mixture in the center of each tortilla, top with ½ cup (15 g) of the spinach and one-fourth of the cauliflower-chickpea mixture. Fold the top and bottom in and roll the sides over to form a burrito.

8. Heat a large, flat griddle over medium heat. Add the burritos and crisp on both sides, about 4 minutes per side or until browned and crispy.

9. To serve, cut each burrito in half and serve with the chutney and pickled onion.

Food Fact: Spinach is fat free, saturated fat free, cholesterol free, low calorie, a good source of magnesium, an excellent source of fiber, and high in vitamins A and C, iron, and folate

FALL BEAN AND BUTTERNUT SQUASH MINESTRONE

GRAIN FREE, SOY FREE, SUGAR FREE

I crave soup on crisp days. This minestrone, with butternut squash, cannellini beans, and Swiss chard is an autumn delight. It also freezes well, so make a double batch and freeze the leftovers. The "parmesan" is not to be missed: it is the perfect accompaniment to minestrone.

INGREDIENTS

SOUP
1¼ cups (130 g) ditalini pasta

2 tablespoons (30 ml) olive oil

1 sweet onion, diced

2 ribs celery, diced

2 carrots, peeled and diced

6 cloves garlic, minced

1 tablespoon (15 g) tomato paste

2 bay leaves

1 teaspoon dried thyme

1 teaspoon dried oregano

½ teaspoon sea salt

1 teaspoon freshly ground black pepper

One 2-pound (910 g) butternut squash, peeled, seeded, and cut into ½-inch (1.3 cm) cubes

One 28-ounce (784 g) can crushed tomatoes

6 cups (1440 ml) vegetable broth

Two 14-ounce (392 g) cans cannellini beans, drained and rinsed

2 cups (60 g) rainbow Swiss chard, cut into ribbons

1 tablespoon (2 g) chopped fresh rosemary

CASHEW PARMESAN
1 cup (140 g) raw cashews

¼ cup (10 g) nutritional yeast

1 teaspoon sea salt

1 teaspoon garlic powder

Food Fact: Butternut Squash is fat free, cholesterol free, sodium free, as well as a good source of fiber, potassium and magnesium. It is an excellent source of vitamins A and C

METHOD OF PREPARATION

1. To make the soup, heat the olive oil in a large Dutch oven over medium heat. Add the onion, celery, and carrots and cook until softened, about 3 minutes.

2. Stir in the garlic, tomato paste, bay leaves, thyme, oregano, salt, and pepper. Stir for 1 minute or until fragrant and well combined.

3. Add the butternut squash, crushed tomatoes, and vegetable broth and bring the soup to a simmer. Cover, decrease the heat to medium-low, and simmer for 15 to 20 minutes or until the squash is tender.

4. Add the cannellini beans, Swiss chard, and rosemary, stir, and adjust the seasonings. Cook for an additional 5 minutes.

5. While the soup finishes, make the cashew parmesan. In the bowl of a food processor, add the cashews, nutritional yeast, salt, and garlic powder. Blend until it resembles grated parmesan cheese, about 1 minute.

6. Ladle the soup into bowls and top with the cashew parmesan.

SWEET POTATO LATKES WITH CHIVES

SERVES 4

GLUTEN FREE, GRAIN FREE, NUT FREE, SOY FREE, SUGAR FREE

INGREDIENTS

2 medium sweet potatoes,
   about 2 pounds (910 g) total, peeled

1 russet potato, peeled

1 sweet onion

1 teaspoon sea salt

½ teaspoon freshly ground black pepper

3 tablespoons (24 g) potato starch

1½ teaspoons chickpea flour

¼ cup (60 ml) grapeseed oil

¼ cup (12 g) minced chives

The latke is a not-to-be-missed fall and holiday side dish. These are made with sweet potato as the star, but the russet potato can be used in its place for a more traditional potato pancake.

METHOD OF PREPARATION

1. Using the fine shredding attachment on the food processor, shred the sweet potatoes, russet potato, and onion. Transfer to a large bowl.

2. Use paper towels or a clean dish towel to squeeze some of the excess water from the potatoes. Discard the water.

3. Add the salt, pepper, starch, and flour to the potatoes and mix well.

4. Heat a cast-iron skillet over medium heat. Add the oil. Once hot, add ¼ cup (60 g) or generous spoonful of the potato mixture to the oil and press down to flatten.

5. Cook for 3 to 5 minutes per side. If the potatoes start to brown too quickly, turn down the heat a little.

6. Drain on paper towels and then place on a platter. Sprinkle with the chives and serve hot or at room temperature.

ROASTED CAULIFLOWER-PARSNIP SOUP WITH MUSHROOMS

SERVES 6

GLUTEN FREE, GRAIN FREE, SOY FREE, SUGAR FREE

This elegant soup is a wonderful and filling one that will impress your family and guests alike. The complexity of the creamy parsnip soup with the thyme and mushrooms is quite unique.

INGREDIENTS

4 cups (400 g) cauliflower florets

5 tablespoons (45 ml) olive oil, divided

One 14-ounce (392 g) can chickpeas, rinsed, drained, and dried

2 cups (140 g) thinly sliced fresh gourmet mushrooms, such as cremini, shiitake, royal trumpet, and oyster

¼ cup (10 g) fresh sage leaves, chiffonade

1¼ teaspoons sea salt, divided

1 cup (160 g) diced sweet onion

4 cloves garlic, minced

4 medium parsnips, peeled and chopped, tough core discarded

1 tablespoon (3 g) dried thyme

4 cups (960 ml) vegetable broth

1½ cups (360 ml) unsweetened almond milk

½ teaspoon freshly ground black pepper

2 tablespoons (30 g) vegan butter, such as Miyoko's

METHOD OF PREPARATION

1. Preheat the oven to 425°F (220°C). Line three baking sheets with parchment paper.

2. On one baking sheet, add the cauliflower and drizzle with 1 tablespoon (15 ml) of the oil. On the second baking sheet, add the dried chickpeas and drizzle with 1 tablespoon (15 ml) of oil. On the third baking sheet, add the sliced mushrooms, drizzle with 1 tablespoon (15 ml) of oil, sprinkle with ¼ teaspoon of the salt, and toss to coat.

3. Transfer all three baking sheets to the oven and roast until super crispy and caramelized, 25 to 30 minutes. Check all of them at 20 minutes.

Food Fact: Mushrooms are fat and saturated fat free, very low in sodium, cholesterol free, low calorie, high in riboflavin, and a good source of niacin, copper, pantothenate, and selenium

4. While the vegetables are roasting, heat the remaining 2 tablespoons (30 ml) olive oil in a large Dutch oven over medium heat. Add the onion and sauté until translucent, about 3 minutes. Add the garlic and stir for 30 seconds.

5. Add the parsnips, thyme, and broth and bring to a boil. Decrease the heat, cover, and simmer for 20 minutes or until the parsnips are tender.

ROASTED DELICATA SQUASH, POMEGRANATE, PEPITA, AND QUINOA SALAD

SERVES 6

INGREDIENTS

2 delicate squash, cut in half lengthwise, seeds removed, and cut into ½-inch (1.3 cm) half-moons

3 tablespoons (45 ml) extra virgin olive oil, divided

1 tablespoon (15 ml) maple syrup

¾ teaspoon sea salt, divided

¾ teaspoon freshly ground black pepper, divided

½ cup (85 g) quinoa

1 cup (240 ml) vegetable broth

1 tablespoon (11 g) Dijon mustard

1 tablespoon (15 ml) maple syrup

¼ cup (60 ml) balsamic vinegar

5 ounces (140 g) baby purple kale

1 cup (140 g) pomegranate arils

¼ cup (35 g) roasted and salted pepitas

Food Fact: Delicata squash is fat free, saturated fat free, cholesterol free, sodium free, an excellent source of vitamin A, and a good source of vitamin C

This salad is an easy packable lunch or an impressive addition to a family get-together. The half-moons of caramelized squash, the protein-packed quinoa, the pop of the pomegranate arils, the salty crunch of the pepitas, and the unique baby purple kale make this not only appealing to the eye but oh so healthy and satisfying.

METHOD OF PREPARATION

1. Preheat the oven to 400°F (200°C). Line a baking sheet with parchment paper and set aside.

2. In a large bowl, toss the squash with 1 tablespoon (15 ml) of the olive oil, the maple syrup, ¼ teaspoon of the salt, and ¼ teaspoon of the pepper. Place on the prepared baking sheet and bake for 18 to 20 minutes or until tender and caramelized. Cool slightly.

3. While the squash is roasting, make the quinoa. In a small saucepan over medium heat, add the quinoa and vegetable broth. Bring to boil, decrease the heat to a simmer, cover, and cook for 15 minutes. Turn off the heat and allow to cook an additional 5 minutes. Cool slightly.

4. In a large salad bowl, combine the Dijon, maple syrup, vinegar, remaining ½ teaspoon salt, and remaining ½ teaspoon pepper. Whisk to combine and then slowly drizzle in the remaining 2 tablespoons (30 ml) olive oil and whisk until incorporated.

5. Add the kale, pomegranate arils, pepitas, cooled squash, and quinoa. Toss to coat in the dressing.

ROASTED BRUSSELS SPROUTS WITH DRIED FIGS, FURIKAKE, AND SLIVERED ALMONDS

SERVES 4

GLUTEN FREE, GRAIN FREE

I had these delicious and distinctive Brussels sprouts at a restaurant recently and decided I had to recreate them. Furikake (pictured) is a dry Japanese seasoning that is sprinkled on top of rice or vegetables. It typically consists of a mixture of sesame seeds, seaweed, sugar, salt, and dried fish… and that's why we are making our own! The dried sweet figs with the Brussels sprouts make this side dish one of a kind and incredibly addictive.

INGREDIENTS

1 pound (455 g) Brussels sprouts, halved

1 cup (150 g) Turkish figs, stems removed, cut into quarters

1 tablespoon (15 ml) toasted sesame oil

1 tablespoon (15 ml) maple syrup

1 tablespoon (15 ml) mirin

½ teaspoon sea salt

½ teaspoon freshly ground black pepper

½ cup (60 g) toasted sliced almonds

FURIKAKE

3 tablespoons (24 g) black sesame seeds

3 tablespoons (24 g) white sesame seeds

20 seasoned snack-size nori seaweed

½ teaspoon raw cane sugar

1 tablespoon (2 g) dulse seaweed flakes

1 tablespoon (15 ml) tamari

1 teaspoon mirin

½ teaspoon toasted sesame oil

Food Fact: Brussels sprouts are low fat, saturated fat free, very low sodium, cholesterol free, low calorie, a good source of dietary fiber and folate, and high in vitamin C

METHOD OF PREPARATION

1. Preheat the oven to 250°F (120°C). Line a baking sheet with parchment paper; set aside.

2. To make the furikake, in the bowl of a food processor, combine the black and white sesame seeds, nori, sugar, and dulse. Pulse 10 times until chopped. Add the tamari, mirin, and sesame oil and pulse until just combined. Spread on the prepared baking sheet.

3. Transfer to the oven and bake for 15 to 20 minutes, stirring every 5 minutes. Let cool completely. The furikake may be stored in an airtight container in the refrigerator for up to 3 weeks.

4. Increase the oven to 450°F (230°C). Line a baking sheet with parchment paper; set aside.

5. In a large bowl, combine the Brussels sprouts, figs, sesame oil, maple syrup, mirin, salt, and pepper. Toss to evenly coat. Spread on the prepared baking sheet in a single later and transfer to the oven.

6. Roast for 20 to 25 minutes, stirring halfway through the cooking time, until charred and caramelized.

7. Remove from the oven and transfer to a platter. Toss with 3 to 4 tablespoons (24 to 32 g) of the furikake and the toasted almonds. Serve hot or cold.

POTATO AND PARSNIP MASH WITH GRAVY SERVES 4

GLUTEN FREE, SOY FREE, SUGAR FREE

INGREDIENTS

4 medium russet potatoes, peeled and chopped

3 parsnips, peeled and chopped

4 cloves garlic, peeled

¼ cup (60 ml) unsweetened almond
   or cashew milk

2 tablespoons (30 ml) olive oil

1 teaspoon sea salt

½ teaspoon freshly ground black pepper

2 tablespoon (15 ml) olive oil

¼ cup (16 g) chopped fresh parsley (optional)

GRAVY

3 tablespoons (45 ml) olive or avocado oil
   or a blend of the two

3 tablespoons (24 g) brown rice flour

1 teaspoon black pepper

1 cup (240 ml) good-quality vegetable stock

¼ teaspoon sea salt

Mashed potatoes: is there anything more comforting and hearty? These are taken a step further with the combination of potatoes and parsnips and a homemade gravy. This dish is perfect paired with the Portobello Mushroom Wellingtons (page 150) or the Lentil and Mushroom Loaf with Glaze (page 120).

METHOD OF PREPARATION

1. Fill a large pot with cold salted water, add the potatoes, parsnips, and garlic, and bring to a boil over high heat. Decrease the heat to medium-high and boil until tender, 15 to 20 minutes. Drain well.

2. While the potatoes and parsnips are cooking, make the gravy. In a medium saucepan, heat the oil over medium heat. Add the flour and black pepper, quickly whisking to make a paste. Stir the flour mixture until lightly browned, about 3 minutes. Whisk in the stock, stirring until the sauce is well combined. Bring to a simmer and then decrease the heat to medium-low. Cook until the gravy is thickened and the flour taste has cooked out, about 3 minutes longer.

3. Once the potatoes are done, use a ricer or a handheld mixer to whip with the milk and 2 tablespoons (30 ml) olive oil. Season with the salt and pepper.

4. To serve, top the whipped parsnip and potato mixture with the gravy and garnish with the parsley, if desired.

LENTIL AND MUSHROOM LOAF WITH GLAZE SERVES 10

GRAIN FREE, NUT FREE, SOY FREE

This loaf is a little time-consuming, but definitely worth the extra effort. I do not recommend substituting canned lentils for the dried ones, as they are a little too mushy and do not give the final dish the desired texture. You may substitute flaxseeds for the chia seeds, though.

INGREDIENTS

LOAF

1 cup (192 g) dried green lentils

3 cups (720 ml) vegetable broth

1 tablespoon (8 g) ground chia seeds

3 tablespoons (45 ml) water

1 sweet onion, roughly chopped

3 large carrots, peeled and roughly chopped

8 ounces (225 g) cremini mushrooms, roughly chopped

2 tablespoons (30 ml) avocado oil

4 cloves garlic, minced

1 teaspoon sea salt

½ teaspoon freshly ground black pepper

Food Fact: Onions are low calorie, high in vitamin C, rich in B vitamins, including folate and B6, and a good source of potassium

1 cup (80 g) old-fashioned rolled oats

½ cup (75 g) sunflower seeds

1 cup (100 g) panko breadcrumbs

¼ cup (60 g) tomato paste

3 tablespoons (45 ml) vegan Worcestershire sauce

2 tablespoons (6 g) dried oregano

2 tablespoons (6 g) dried thyme

GLAZE

½ cup (120 g) organic ketchup

¼ cup (44 g) yellow mustard

2 tablespoons (30 ml) maple syrup

1 tablespoon (15 ml) vegan Worcestershire sauce

METHOD OF PREPARATION

1. To make the loaf, in a medium saucepan over medium-high heat, combine the lentils and broth. Bring to a boil, decrease the heat to low, and simmer, uncovered, for 30 minutes. Once the lentils are tender, drain, transfer to a large bowl, and set aside to cool.

2. Meanwhile, preheat the oven to 375°F (190°C). Line two 9 x 5 x 3-inch (23 x 12.5 x 7.5 cm) or 8½ x 4½ x 2½-inch (21.6 x 11.4 x 6.3 cm) loaf pans with parchment paper, allowing it to hang over all sides for easy removal after baking.

3. In a small bowl, combine the chia seeds and water, stir, and set aside.

4. In the bowl of a food processor, add the onion, carrot, and mushrooms. Pulse until finely chopped.

5. In a large sauté pan over medium heat, add the avocado oil. Add the chopped vegetables and sauté for 3 minutes, stirring occasionally, until translucent. Stir in the garlic, salt, and pepper. Set aside to cool slightly.

6. In the bowl of the food processor, add half of the lentils and puree until smooth. Add back to the bowl with the whole lentils. Add the sautéed vegetables to the bowl as well.

7. In the bowl of the same food processor, combine the oats and sunflower seeds. Pulse until finely chopped. Add to the vegetable mixture along with the panko.

8. In a small bowl, mix together the tomato paste, Worcestershire, oregano, thyme, and chia mixture. Add to the lentil mixture and mix to combine.

9. Divide the mixture between the prepared loaf pans and smooth the top.

10. To make the glaze, in a medium bowl, combine the ketchup, mustard, maple syrup, and Worcestershire; whisk until smooth.

11. Divide the glaze between the loaves and pour over the top.

12. Transfer to the oven and bake for 45 minutes.

13. Allow to cool for 15 minutes before removing the loaves from the pans. Slice to serve.

DECADENT CHOCOLATE-ON-CHOCOLATE CAKE SERVES 16

GRAIN FREE, SOY FREE

This super simple rich chocolate cake is going to become your go-to fall dessert. You can make it into cupcakes too, just check the cakes at around 18 to 20 minutes. The boiling water ensures a moist and tender cake.

INGREDIENTS

CAKE

Coconut oil spray

2 cups (240 g) unbleached all-purpose flour

2 cups (400 g) organic raw cane sugar

¾ cup (90 g) unsweetened dark cocoa powder

2 teaspoons baking powder

1½ teaspoons baking soda

1 teaspoon kosher salt

1 teaspoon espresso powder

1 cup (240 ml) unsweetened almond milk

1 teaspoon apple cider vinegar

½ cup (120 ml) coconut oil, melted

6 tablespoons (90 ml) aquafaba (see page 54), lightly whipped

2 teaspoons vanilla extract

1 cup (240 ml) boiling water

FROSTING

1 cup (120 g) unsweetened dark cocoa powder

1½ cups (360 g) vegan butter, such as Miyoko's, softened

5 cups (600 g) organic powdered sugar

½ cup (120 ml) unsweetened almond milk

2 teaspoons vanilla extract

½ teaspoon espresso powder

METHOD OF PREPARATION

1. Preheat the oven to 350°F (180°C). Coat two 9-inch (23 cm) cake pans with coconut oil spray and lightly flour. Tap out the excess flour and set aside.

2. To make the cake, add the flour, cane sugar, cocoa, baking powder, baking soda, salt, and espresso powder to a large bowl or the bowl of a stand mixer. Whisk to combine or, using your paddle attachment, stir through the flour mixture until well combined.

3. In a liquid measuring cup, mix together the almond milk and apple cider vinegar. Let stand for 1 minute. Add melted coconut, the aquafaba, and vanilla and whisk to combine. It is okay if the coconut oil congeals a little.

4. Add the liquids to the dry ingredients and mix together on medium speed until well combined. Reduce the speed and carefully add the boiling water to the batter until well combined.

5. Divide the cake batter evenly between the two prepared cake pans. Bake for 25 to 30 minutes, until a toothpick or cake tester inserted in the center of the cake comes out clean.

6. Remove from the oven and allow to cool for about 10 minutes. Remove the cakes from the pans and cool completely on a wire rack.

7. Make the frosting while the cake cools. Add the cocoa powder to the bowl of a stand mixer. Whisk thoroughly to remove any lumps.

8. Add the softened butter and cream together.

9. Add the powdered sugar and almond milk to the cocoa mixture by adding 1 cup (120 g) of sugar followed by a little milk. Beat to combine, then turn the mixer to high speed and beat for about 1 minute. Repeat until all the sugar and milk have been added.

10. Add the vanilla and espresso powder and mix until well combined.

11. If the frosting appears too dry, add more milk, 1 tablespoon (15 ml) at a time, until it reaches the right consistency. If it appears too wet and does not hold its form, add more powdered sugar, 1 tablespoon (8 g) at a time, until it reaches the right consistency.

12. Once the cake is completely cooled, frost it. Invert one cake on a cake stand or platter. Apply half of the frosting and spread. Add the other cake on top and spread the other half of the frosting over it. Store this cake in the refrigerator... if there is any left!

PUMPKIN, CASHEW CHEESECAKE WITH PHYLLO CRUST

SERVES 16

GRAIN FREE

Oh man, is this one requested fall dessert! The phyllo crust gives this cheesecake a unique and lighter spin to the traditional crust. The filling is not too sweet, so creamy, and incredibly addictive. Your guests will be trying to guess the ingredients… is there banana? Is that orange? It's so complex!

INGREDIENTS

CRUST
¾ cup (150 g) raw cane sugar or coconut sugar

1 teaspoon ground cinnamon

8 sheets phyllo dough, thawed

1 cup (240 ml) coconut oil, melted

FILLING
½ cup (70 g) raw cashews, soaked in water for 2 to 8 hours, drained, and rinsed

¼ cup (60 g) mashed ripe banana

One 14-ounce (392 g) package silken tofu

½ cup (100 g) coconut sugar

⅓ cup (65 g) brown coconut sugar

3 tablespoons (45 ml) coconut oil, melted

2 tablespoons (16 g) cornstarch

2 tablespoons (30 ml) freshly squeezed lemon juice

1 tablespoon (15 ml) vanilla extract

½ teaspoon grated orange zest

¼ teaspoon sea salt

1¼ cups (300 g) canned pumpkin puree

1 teaspoon ground cinnamon

½ teaspoon ground ginger

¼ teaspoon ground nutmeg

Food Fact: Pumpkin is fat free, cholesterol free, sodium free, a good source of vitamin C, and an excellent source of vitamin A

(continued on page 126)

(continued from page 124)

METHOD OF PREPARATION

1. Preheat the oven to 400°F (200°C). Line a baking sheet with foil. Have a 9-inch (23 cm) springform pan ready.

2. To make the crust, in a small bowl, combine the sugar and cinnamon.

3. Brush 1 sheet of phyllo dough with the melted coconut oil (as you work, keep the remaining phyllo dough covered with a damp kitchen towel) and sprinkle with the sugar mixture.

4. Starting at one short end, fold the phyllo in half over the coconut oil mixture and brush with more coconut oil. Transfer to the springform pan, oil-side down, gently pressing into the bottom and sides.

5. Repeat with the 7 sheets of remaining phyllo, coconut oil, and sugar mixture, arranging in overlapping layers to completely and evenly cover the bottom and sides of the pan.

6. Place on the prepared baking sheet to catch any drippings. Transfer to the oven and bake for 15 to 20 minutes or until crisp and golden. Let cool while you make the filling.

7. Decrease the oven temperature to 350°F (180°C).

8. To make the filling, in a high-powered blender, combine the drained and rinsed cashews, banana, tofu, coconut sugar, brown sugar, coconut oil, cornstarch, lemon juice, vanilla, zest, and salt. Blend until smooth and creamy, about 1 minute. Add the pumpkin and spices and blend until smooth.

9. Pour into the prepared crust and transfer to the oven. Bake for 45 to 50 minutes. The cheesecake will be done when the top is lightly puffed and the edges are golden. Remove from the oven and allow to cool for 20 minutes. Transfer to the refrigerator and chill for 4 hours or up to overnight.

10. To serve, remove the springform, dip a knife in ice water, and slice.

STICKY ORANGE AND VANILLA UPSIDE-DOWN CAKE

SERVES 8 TO 12

GRAIN FREE, SOY FREE

An upside-down cake is so aesthetically pleasing and equally as delicious. This one combines vanilla and orange for a delightful spin on the classic. The addition of almond meal adds another layer of unexpected flavor and texture.

INGREDIENTS

SYRUP AND CANDIED ORANGES

¾ cup (180 ml) water

½ cup (100 g) coconut sugar

2 oranges, washed and thinly sliced, seeds removed (rind on)

1 vanilla bean, split and scraped

Food Fact: Oranges are fat free, saturated fat free, sodium free, cholesterol free, a good source of dietary fiber, and high in vitamin C

CAKE

1 large orange

1 cup (120 g) unbleached all-purpose flour

½ cup (60 g) almond meal

½ cup (100 g) coconut sugar or organic raw cane sugar

¼ teaspoon sea salt

1 teaspoon baking powder

½ teaspoon baking soda

½ cup (120 ml) coconut oil, melted

1 teaspoon white vinegar

(continued on page 128)

(continued from page 127)

METHOD OF PREPARATION

1. Preheat the oven to 350°F (180°C). Lightly oil an 8-inch (20 cm) cake pan; set aside.

2. To make the syrup and candied oranges, in a medium saucepan over medium-high heat, add the water and sugar and stir until the sugar is completely dissolved. Add the sliced oranges and vanilla bean seeds and pods. Decrease the heat to low and simmer for 20 to 30 minutes. The rinds will be softened, and the liquid will be a sticky syrup.

3. Meanwhile, make the cake batter. Grate the large orange peel and reserve the zest. Then peel the orange and add the flesh to a high-powered blender and puree until smooth. You should have 1 cup (240 ml) of orange juice. Add water to make 1 cup (240 ml) if it's shy.

4. In a large bowl, whisk together the orange zest, flour, almond meal, coconut sugar, salt, baking powder, and baking soda.

5. In a medium bowl, whisk together the orange juice, coconut oil, and vinegar.

6. Make a well in the center of the dry ingredients and add the wet ingredients. Whisk until just combined. The dough will be thick and sticky.

7. To assemble, arrange the softened rinds in a concentric circle in the prepared pan. Pour the syrup over the top.

8. Pour the batter over the rinds.

9. Transfer to the oven and bake for 35 to 40 minutes or until the cake pulls away from the sides and a toothpick inserted in the center comes out clean. Let cool for 5 minutes.

10. Carefully place a large platter over the cake pan, turn the pan upside down, tap the bottom, and release the cake. Serve warm.

PEAR TARTE TATIN

GRAIN FREE, NUT FREE, SOY FREE

This pretty classic is equally easy to make as it is impressive to guests. You could make this with apples as well. Serve warm with a little whipped coconut cream (page 35 or page 132) or your favorite almond, cashew, or soy vanilla bean ice cream.

INGREDIENTS

½ cup (100 g) coconut sugar

2 tablespoons (30 ml) water

3 tablespoons (45 g) vegan butter, such as Miyoko's

2 tablespoons (30 ml) freshly squeezed lemon juice

4 Anjou or Bartlett pears, ripe but firm

1 vegan puff pastry sheet, thawed

Food Fact: Pears are fat free, saturated fat free, sodium free, cholesterol free, an excellent source of dietary fiber, and a good source of vitamin C

METHOD OF PREPARATION

1. Preheat the oven to 375°F (190°C).

2. In a 10-inch (25 cm) cast-iron skillet, stir together the sugar and water. Cook over medium heat, without stirring, until the mixture turns golden brown, about 5 minutes. Stir in the butter. Stir in the lemon juice.

3. While the sugar mixture is cooking, peel the pears and cut in half, then quarters, remove the cores, and then cut the halves lengthwise into 2 thick slices (8 slices per pear).

4. When the caramel is ready, arrange the pear slices in concentric circles. Turn the heat to medium-low and cook for 3 to 4 minutes or until the pears are tender.

5. Lay the pastry out on a clean, dry surface. Cut the pastry into a circle slightly bigger than the pan you are using, about 11 inches (28 cm). Prick the pastry randomly with a fork. Place the pastry over the top of the pears, tucking the overlap into the pan.

6. Transfer to the oven and bake for 25 to 30 minutes or until the pastry is puffed and golden.

7. Place the pan on a wire rack and allow to cool for 15 minutes.

8. Run a knife around the edges of the skillet. Place a serving platter on top of the pan, and carefully invert the tart onto the platter. Allow to cool for 5 minutes longer and then serve warm with whipped coconut cream if desired.

DOUBLE HOT CHOCOLATE
WITH WHIPPED COCONUT CREAM

SERVES 2

GLUTEN FREE, GRAIN FREE, NUT FREE, RAW, SOY FREE

INGREDIENTS

WHIPPED COCONUT CREAM

One 14-ounce (392 g) can full-fat coconut milk, refrigerated for at least 24 hours

2 tablespoons (25 g) coconut sugar

1 teaspoon vanilla extract

HOT CHOCOLATE

One 14-ounce (392 g) can light coconut milk

2 tablespoons (16 g) unsweetened cocoa powder

2 tablespoons (30 ml) maple syrup

½ teaspoon vanilla extract

½ teaspoon ground espresso

⅛ teaspoon Himalayan pink sea salt

¼ cup (45 g) dairy-free semisweet chocolate chips

Crisp fall day, thick chunky sweater, a great book, and this hot chocolate. Sounds like the perfect fall day to me! This hot chocolate is divine, so rich and so creamy.

METHOD OF PREPARATION

1. To make the whipped coconut cream, place your mixing bowl in the freezer for 10 minutes.

2. Once your bowl is cold, remove the can of cold full-fat coconut milk from the refrigerator. Carefully remove the top of the can; do not shake or tip upside down. Scoop the thick layer of coconut cream from the top of the can, leaving the water at the bottom for another use.

3. Using a whisk attachment, beat the coconut cream on medium speed for 2 to 4 minutes, or until the cream becomes light and fluffy and peaks form. Add the sugar and vanilla and beat until just incorporated.

4. To make the hot chocolate, in a high-speed blender, combine the light coconut milk, cocoa powder, maple syrup, vanilla, espresso, and salt. Blend on high speed for a few minutes until completely smooth and frothy. Make sure you blend for the full 3 minutes, because it needs to become light and frothy.

5. Add the mixture to a small saucepan over medium heat. Add the chocolate chips and whisk for about 4 minutes or until it thickens and is just beginning to bubble.

6. Pour into two mugs, dollop some coconut cream on top, and serve.

BAKED APPLE CIDER DOUGHNUTS

GRAIN FREE, NUT FREE, SOY FREE

INGREDIENTS

Coconut oil spray

1 cup (120 g) unbleached all-purpose flour

1½ teaspoons baking powder

½ teaspoon baking soda

½ teaspoon ground cinnamon

⅛ teaspoon ground nutmeg

⅛ teaspoon ground allspice

½ teaspoon kosher salt

⅓ cup (80 ml) maple syrup

⅓ cup (80 ml) apple cider

¼ cup (60 g) applesauce

1 tablespoon (15 ml) coconut oil, melted

1 teaspoon vanilla extract

TOPPING

¼ cup (50 g) organic raw cane sugar

2 teaspoons ground cinnamon

Apple cider doughnuts scream fall farmer's market to me. The smell of these baking is just delectable. You might want to invest in a couple more doughnut pans because six of these will disappear as quickly as you can make them.

METHOD OF PREPARATION

1. Preheat the oven to 350°F (180°C). Coat a doughnut pan with coconut oil spray and set aside.

2. In a medium bowl, combine the flour, baking powder, baking soda, cinnamon, nutmeg, allspice, and salt. Whisk to combine.

3. In another medium bowl, whisk together the maple syrup, apple cider, applesauce, coconut oil, and vanilla.

4. Add the wet ingredients to the dry and mix until just combined.

5. Spoon the batter into the prepared doughnut pan, filling them ¾ full.

6. Transfer to the oven and bake for 8 to 10 minutes or until the doughnuts spring back to the touch. Allow to cool in the pan for 5 minutes, then transfer to a wire rack.

7. Meanwhile, make the topping. Whisk together the sugar and cinnamon.

8. When the doughnuts have cooled slightly, dip them into the sugar mixture and serve warm!

DRACULA'S LOVE POTION

GLUTEN FREE, GRAIN FREE, NUT FREE, RAW, SOY FREE, SUGAR FREE, UNPROCESSED

INGREDIENTS

1 cup (240 g) frozen dragon fruit

1 cup (240 g) frozen strawberries

1 cup (240 g) frozen raspberries

½ cup (120 g) frozen cherries

1 beet, peeled and chopped

½ cup (70 g) pomegranate arils

1 tablespoon (15 ml) rose water

2 cups (480 ml) water

Food Fact: Beets are fat free, saturated fat free, cholesterol free, low sodium, and an excellent source of folate

I had to throw in a fall Halloween treat. This blood-red drink is not only spooky but also incredibly nutritious and delicious. Get creative in how you serve it, like in these glass or plastic test tubes.

METHOD OF PREPARATION

1. Add all the ingredients to a high-powered blender. Blend on high speed until smooth and creamy.

2. Serve in test tubes or beakers for an extra special and scary Halloween treat!

PEANUT BUTTER CARAMEL APPLES

GLUTEN FREE, GRAIN FREE, SOY FREE

INGREDIENTS

6 popsicle or craft sticks

1 cup (240 ml) sweetened condensed
  coconut milk

1 cup (240 g) organic creamy peanut butter
  or almond butter

½ teaspoon sea salt

6 crispy apples, such as Granny Smith,
  Honeycrisp, Gala, or your favorite

1 cup (140 g) chopped salted peanuts

Caramel apples are the quintessential fall
treat, and these are made doubly enjoyable
with peanut butter. These take a little planning
because they require overnight refrigeration.

METHOD OF PREPARATION

1. Line a baking sheet with parchment paper;
set aside.

2. In a medium saucepan over medium heat,
add the condensed milk, nut butter, and salt.
Whisk well to combine. Stirring constantly,
bring to a simmer; turn off the heat.

3. Stick a popsicle stick or sturdy craft stick
into the center of each apple. Dip the apples
into the peanut butter mixture, then roll in the
chopped nuts.

4. Place the dipped apples on the prepared
baking sheet and transfer to the refrigerator
overnight. Store in the fridge until ready
to serve.

GRANOLA-STUFFED BAKED APPLES WITH APPLE CIDER SAUCE

SERVES 4

GLUTEN FREE, GRAIN FREE, SOY FREE, UNPROCESSED

INGREDIENTS

4 medium apples, such as Honeycrisp

2 cups (400 g) dried fruit and nut granola

¼ cup (60 ml) maple syrup

¼ cup (60 ml) coconut butter, melted

1½ cups (360 ml) fresh apple cider

Baked apples are a healthy and comforting dessert, especially when stuffed with granola. Buy a great-quality granola because it is the star in this simple dessert.

METHOD OF PREPARATION

1. Preheat the oven to 425°F (220°C). Line a 9 x 13-inch (23 x 33 cm) baking dish with foil and set aside.

2. Cut the apples in half, cutting through the stem and bottom. Scoop out the core, seeds, and some of the pulp, leaving a ¼-inch (6 mm) shell. Place the apples in the prepared baking dish.

3. In a medium bowl, stir together the granola, maple syrup, and coconut butter. Spoon the granola mixture into the apple halves. Pour the apple cider around the apples and cover the pan with foil.

4. Transfer the baking dish to the oven and bake for 10 minutes. Remove the foil and bake for an additional 10 to 15 minutes or until the apples are tender.

5. To serve, transfer the apples to a bowl and spoon the sauce over.

CHOCOLATE-COVERED
PUMPKIN CAKE POPS

SERVES 12

GLUTEN FREE, GRAIN FREE, SOY FREE

These simple cake pops are not only tasty but also healthy and so cute! The cake is a nutritious blend of pumpkin, dates, sunflower, coconut, and spices and then covered in dark chocolate. Serve as a snack or dessert.

INGREDIENTS

CAKE

½ cup (75 g) raw unsalted sunflower seeds

½ cup (40 g) unsweetened coconut flakes

10 Medjool dates, pitted

¼ cup (60 g) canned pumpkin puree

1 tablespoon (8 g) almond flour

¼ teaspoon sea salt

½ teaspoon ground cinnamon

¼ teaspoon ground nutmeg

¼ teaspoon vanilla extract

COATING

½ cup (85 g) dairy-free dark chocolate chips

½ cup (120 ml) unsweetened coconut flakes

12 cake pop sticks

Food Fact: Coconut is high in calories, high in plant-based saturated fat, high in fiber, an excellent source of manganese and copper, and a good source of selenium, potassium, iron, and zinc

METHOD OF PREPARATION

1. Line a baking sheet with parchment paper; set aside.

2. To make the cake, in the bowl of a food processor, combine the sunflower seeds, coconut flakes, dates, pumpkin puree, almond flour, salt, cinnamon, nutmeg, and vanilla. Pulse to combine. Then turn the processor on high and process until the mixture is well combined. Scrape down the bowl occasionally if needed.

3. Using a tablespoon-size scoop, scoop the dough, roll it into a ball, and place on the prepared baking sheet. Repeat the process with the remaining dough. Refrigerate for 30 minutes.

4. After the cake pops have chilled, make the coating by melting the chocolate in a double boiler.

5. Put a stick in each cake pop. Dip the cake bites in the melted chocolate to coat and repeat with the remaining bites, placing the chocolate-coated ones back on the parchment paper.

6. Pour the coconut flakes onto a small plate and before the chocolate has hardened, dip the bottom into the coconut.

7. Transfer back to the baking sheet and refrigerate for at least 30 minutes.

8. Store in an airtight container in the refrigerator for up to 5 days.

WINTER RECIPES

FRUITS & VEGETABLES IN SEASON

Beets • Belgium Endive • Broccoli • Brussels Sprouts

Butternut Squash • Cactus Pear • Cardoon • Cauliflower

Celery Root • Cherimoya • Clementines • Collard Greens

Dates • Delicata Squash • Escarole • Fennel • Grapefruit

Jerusalem Artichokes • Kale • Kiwi • Kumquat • Leeks

Mandarin Oranges • Maradol Papaya • Meyer Lemon

Oranges • Passion Fruit • Pear • Persimmons

Pomegranate • Pomelo • Red Currants • Romanesco

Sweet Potatoes • Tangerines • Turnips

CRISPY BAKED VEGAN MAC AND CHEESE

SUGAR FREE

INGREDIENTS

Olive oil or coconut oil spray

1½ cups (360 ml) almond, cashew,
   or hemp milk

1½ cups (60 g) nutritional yeast

1 cup (240 ml) olive oil

⅓ cup (80 ml) tamari, soy sauce,
   or Bragg's liquid aminos

3 ounces (84 g) firm tofu, drained

1 teaspoon Dijon mustard

1 tablespoon (18 g) salt

1 pound (455 g) elbow pasta, brown rice,
   or quinoa, cooked according to the package
   directions, drained

1 cup (115 g) panko breadcrumbs

2 tablespoons (30 g) vegan butter, such as
   Miyoko's, diced

Mac and cheese… let's be honest, there are no vegetables in this dish, but I couldn't leave it out of our winter recipes. It's comfort food fair and square, and this one is creamy and crunchy and satisfying when the mac and cheese craving hits. The sauce is simply made in the blender. Baking it is optional, but the crunchy topping truly does make this extra special.

METHOD OF PREPARATION

1. Preheat the oven to 400°F (200°C). Spray an 8 x 8-inch (20 x 20 cm) pan with olive oil or coconut cooking spray and set aside.

2. In a blender, combine the milk, yeast, oil, tamari, tofu, mustard, and salt and puree until smooth and creamy, about 1 minute.

3. In a large bowl, combine the cooked pasta with the sauce.

4. Transfer to the prepared baking dish and top with the panko and diced butter.

5. Transfer to the oven and bake for 10 to 15 minutes or until golden brown and bubbly.

WHOLE HEAD OF ROASTED CAULIFLOWER
WITH TURMERIC TAHINI SAUCE

SERVES 6

GLUTEN FREE, GRAIN FREE, NUT FREE, SOY FREE, SUGAR FREE, UNPROCESSED

INGREDIENTS

1 large head cauliflower

¼ cup (60 ml) olive or blended oil

Kosher salt and pepper

SAUCE

½ cup (120 ml) tahini

¼ cup (60 ml) rice wine vinegar

¼ cup (60 ml) water

1 tablespoon (6 g) turmeric

1 teaspoon sea salt

TO SERVE

½ cup (70 g) pomegranate arils

¼ cup (5 g) chopped fresh parsley

Food Fact: Pomegranates are low in fat, saturated fat free, cholesterol free, sodium free, an excellent source of fiber and vitamins C and K, and a good source of potassium, folate, and copper

I had this dish in New York City once and I have been recreating it ever since. The presentation is insanely beautiful, the crunch from the cauliflower and the arils is delightful, and the creamy sauce poured over the top at the table is exceptional. This is a dish that will wow your guests. Serve it in the cast-iron pan with a steak knife right on the table.

METHOD OF PREPARATION

1. Preheat the oven to 375°F (190°C).

2. Break off and discard the outer leaves from the cauliflower. Cut off the bottom of the stem, creating a flat surface. Rinse the cauliflower and do not dry.

3. Place the cauliflower into a cast-iron skillet and drizzle with the oil and season with salt and pepper.

4. Transfer to the oven and roast for 1 to 1½ hours or until a knife inserted in the center comes out easily.

5. While the cauliflower is roasting, make the sauce. In a blender, combine the tahini, vinegar, water, turmeric, and salt. Blend until smooth and creamy. Set aside.

6. To serve, transfer the cauliflower to a platter, pour the sauce over the top, and sprinkle with the arils and parsley.

PORTOBELLO MUSHROOM WELLINGTONS WITH RED WINE JUS

GRAIN FREE, SOY FREE, SUGAR FREE

This dish is so special. It's elegant and sophisticated and I have been told on many occasions that it blows traditional Wellington out of the water! It takes a little time, but is truly the centerpiece for that winter holiday celebration. I love to serve the red wine jus in a gravy boat to be added by the diner at the table. Serve this with creamy mashed potatoes and crispy green beans for the ultimate pairing.

INGREDIENTS

PORTOBELLO MUSHROOMS

4 portobello mushrooms

1 tablespoon (15 ml) olive oil

½ teaspoon sea salt

½ teaspoon freshly ground black pepper

CREMINI MUSHROOMS

1 pound (455 g) cremini mushrooms, wiped clean and quartered

2 tablespoons (30 ml) olive oil

2 shallots, minced

4 cloves garlic, minced

1 tablespoon (3 g) fresh thyme leaves, minced

½ teaspoon sea salt

¼ teaspoon freshly ground black pepper

2 tablespoons (30 ml) cashew or almond cream

WELLINGTONS

2 vegan puff pastry sheets

1 tablespoon (15 ml) aquafaba (chickpea water)

1 tablespoon (15 ml) unsweetened cashew or almond milk

1 teaspoon olive oil

½ teaspoon maple syrup

JUS

2 cups (480 ml) fruity red wine, such as a Pinot Noir or Beaujolais

1 cup (240 ml) mushroom broth

2 teaspoons date syrup

METHOD OF PREPARATION

1. Arrange a rack in the middle of the oven, and then preheat the oven to 425°F (220°C). Line a baking sheet with parchment paper; set aside.

2. To make the portobello mushrooms, remove the stems and then scrape out the gills with a spoon. Arrange the mushrooms on the prepared baking sheet and season with the olive oil, salt, and pepper. Transfer to the oven and roast for 12 to 15 minutes. Remove from the oven and allow to cool.

3. Reduce the oven temperature to 400°F (200°C).

4. To make the cremini mushrooms, in the bowl of a food processor, add the cremini mushrooms and pulse until coarsely chopped, about 20 pulses.

5. In a large sauté pan over medium heat, add the olive oil. Once hot, add the minced shallots and cook, stirring occasionally, for 2 minutes. Add the garlic and stir.

6. Add the chopped cremini mushrooms and cook until tender, stirring occasionally, until the moisture has evaporated, 6 to 8 minutes. Season with the thyme, salt, and pepper.

7. Stir in the cashew or almond cream and cook for another 2 to 3 minutes or until thick and creamy.

8. To assemble the wellingtons, cut each sheet of puff pastry into two equal pieces. Roll them out with a rolling pin until they are large enough to wrap your portobello mushrooms inside. Place one roasted portobello

mushroom in the center of puff pastry sheet. Divide the cremini mushroom mixture among the portobello mushrooms. Fold the pastry around the mushrooms, gathering the four points together and squeezing them to seal. Place back onto your parchment-lined baking sheet.

9. In a small bowl, whisk together the aquafaba, nut milk, olive oil, and maple syrup. Brush the pastries with the mixture.

10. Transfer to the oven and bake until the pastry is puffed and golden, 25 to 30 minutes.

11. While the Wellingtons are baking, make the jus. In a small saucepan over medium heat, add the red wine and broth. Bring to a simmer, reduce the heat to low, and continue to simmer for 20 minutes or until reduced by half. Stir in the date syrup and keep warm until ready to serve.

12. To serve, arrange the Wellingtons on a platter and allow guests to pour the jus on top.

Food Fact: Portobello mushrooms are low in sodium, and very low in saturated fat and cholesterol. They are a good source of protein, thiamin, vitamin B6, folate, magnesium, zinc, and manganese. They are also a very good source of dietary fiber, riboflavin, niacin, pantothenic acid, phosphorus, potassium, copper, and selenium

CREAMY KALE GRATIN

GLUTEN FREE, SOY FREE, SUGAR FREE

INGREDIENTS

2 tablespoons (30 ml) olive or blended oil

10 ounces (280 g) Tuscan kale, stems removed,
    washed, and roughly chopped

2 tablespoons (30 ml) white wine

Salt and pepper to taste

½ cup (60 g) raw cashews

1 cup (240 ml) water

⅓ cup (14 g) nutritional yeast

1 clove garlic, peeled

2 teaspoons Dijon mustard

¼ cup (35 g) polenta

Food Fact: Kale is low fat, saturated fat free, cholesterol free, low sodium, an excellent source of vitamins A and C, and a good source of calcium and potassium

This gratin is simple to prepare and an elegant addition to any holiday meal. I've made it with regular curly kale, but Tuscan kale is denser and holds up better in this preparation. The polenta adds a nice crunch and soaks up any of the excess liquid. This one always finds its way onto the winter holiday table.

METHOD OF PREPARATION

1. Preheat the oven to 400°F (200°C) and grease a gratin dish or shallow pie dish; set aside.

2. In a large frying pan, add the oil and warm over medium heat. Add the kale and wine. Cover the pan and cook for 3 to 5 minutes or until wilted and tender. Season with salt and pepper.

3. To make the cashew cream, place the cashews, water, nutritional yeast, garlic, and Dijon in a high-powered blender; blend until smooth and creamy.

4. Mix together the cashew cream and kale. Pour into the prepared gratin dish. Sprinkle with the polenta and transfer to the oven. Bake for 20 to 25 minutes or until lightly browned and bubbly.

HASSELBACK BUTTERNUT SQUASH WITH RED CURRANTS AND HAZELNUTS

SERVES 8

GLUTEN FREE, GRAIN FREE, SOY FREE, SUGAR FREE

I love when a dish is extraordinary in both flavor and presentation. This butternut squash is one of those dishes. The caramelized and tender squash topped with the crunch of the hazelnuts and the freshness and pop of the red currants is going to make this a holiday favorite! Again, it's a more time-consuming recipe, but so worth the effort. If you can't find red currants, you could substitute pomegranate arils.

INGREDIENTS

1 large butternut squash

¼ cup (60 ml) water

2 tablespoons (30 ml) avocado oil

1 teaspoon sea salt

½ teaspoon freshly ground black pepper

1 shallot, minced

2 cloves garlic, minced

3 tablespoons (45 ml) maple syrup

2 tablespoons (22 g) Dijon mustard

2 tablespoons (30 ml) apple cider vinegar

½ cup (65) red currants

⅓ cup (45 g) hazelnuts, blanched, toasted, and roughly chopped

⅓ cup (15 g) thinly sliced fresh chives

METHOD OF PREPARATION

1. Preheat the oven to 425°F (220°C). Line a rimmed baking sheet with parchment paper; set aside.

2. Using a vegetable peeler, peel the skin from the butternut squash, leaving the stem intact. Cut the squash in half lengthwise and scoop out the seeds.

3. Place the squash, cut-side down, on the prepared baking sheet and add the water. Transfer to the oven and roast for 20 minutes.

4. Remove the squash from the oven and allow to cool for 10 minutes or until it is cool enough to touch.

Food Fact: Butternut squash is fat free, cholesterol free, sodium free, a good source of fiber, potassium, and magnesium, and an excellent source of vitamins A and C

5. Place the butternut cut-side down on a cutting board; using a sharp knife, cut into thin ⅛ inch (3 mm) slits. Do not cut all the way through. Repeat with the other half. Return the squash halves to the baking sheet.

6. In a small bowl, whisk together the avocado oil, salt, pepper, shallot, garlic, maple syrup, Dijon, and vinegar. Brush the sauce over the top of the butternut, making sure some of it gets down into the cuts you made. Use about half of the sauce to brush.

7. Transfer the squash back to the oven and roast for 30 to 35 minutes or until golden and tender.

8. While the squash is roasting, add the remaining sauce to a small saucepan and place over medium heat until it comes to a simmer. Decrease the heat to low and simmer for 2 to 3 minutes or until slightly thickened.

9. When the squash is done, remove it from the oven and transfer it to a large platter. Pour the reduced sauce over the top and sprinkle with the red currants, hazelnuts, and chives.

LEEK, CHESTNUT, AND
APPLE STUFFED ACORN SQUASH

GRAIN FREE, SOY FREE, SUGAR FREE

Main dish, side dish, who knows? What we do know is this little beauty is the ultimate comfort. I've served this with a side salad for a simple and sophisticated dinner or as a side dish to a holiday spread, and both are fantastic and so satisfying. I love to buy the precooked vacuum-sealed packages of chestnuts because it makes this recipe a little less daunting.

INGREDIENTS

4 acorn squash, about 1 pound (455 g) each, halved lengthwise and seeded

1 teaspoon sea salt

½ teaspoon freshly ground black pepper

1 teaspoon olive oil

STUFFING

2 tablespoons (30 g) vegan butter, such as Miyoko's

3 tablespoons (45 ml) olive oil

2 cups (210 g) cleaned and sliced leeks

2 cups (240 g) diced celery

½ cup (120 ml) white wine

1½ cups (225 g) peeled and diced green apple

4 cloves garlic, minced

2 teaspoons minced fresh thyme

½ teaspoon sea salt

½ teaspoon freshly ground black pepper

4 cups (400 g) cubed day-old whole-wheat sourdough, crusts removed

1 cup (150 g) cooked chestnuts, roughly chopped

¼ cup (35 g) dried cranberries

½ cup (120 ml) cashew or almond cream

½ cup (120 ml) vegetable broth

Food Fact: Acorn squash is fat free, saturated fat free, cholesterol free, sodium free, and a good source of vitamin C

METHOD OF PREPARATION

1. Preheat the oven to 350°F (180°C). Line a baking sheet with parchment paper; set aside.

2. Sprinkle the flesh sides of the acorn squash with the salt and pepper. Place it cut-side down on the prepared baking sheet. Brush the outside with the 1 teaspoon olive oil. Transfer to the oven and bake for 25 to 30 minutes or until just tender.

3. While the squash is roasting, make the stuffing. In a large sauté pan over medium heat, melt the butter with the olive oil. Once hot, add the leeks and celery. Cook, stirring occasionally, until softened, 7 to 8 minutes.

4. Add the white wine and cook for another 3 to 4 minutes or until most of the wine has evaporated.

5. Add the apples, garlic, and thyme and cook for another 5 minutes or until the apples are just tender. Remove from the heat and season with salt and pepper. Transfer to a large bowl.

6. Add the bread, chestnuts, cranberries, cashew or almond cream, and vegetable broth. Stir well.

7. Once the squash has baked, remove from the oven and turn them flesh-side up. Divide the stuffing among the 8 squash halves and return to the oven. Bake for 18 to 20 minutes or until the stuffing is golden brown. Transfer to a platter and serve.

BRUSSELS SPROUTS, APPLE, TURNIP, AND MANDARIN SLAW

GLUTEN FREE, GRAIN FREE, SOY FREE, SUGAR FREE, UNPROCESSED

INGREDIENTS

¼ cup (60 ml) freshly squeezed orange juice

3 tablespoons (45 ml) extra virgin olive oil

1 teaspoon freshly grated ginger

½ teaspoon sea salt

4 ounces (112 g) Brussels sprouts, stems removed and leaves separated

2 mandarin oranges, peeled and segmented

2 small white turnips, peeled and cut into matchsticks

1 medium apple, such as Pink Lady, cut into matchsticks

¼ cup (35 g) pine nuts, toasted

Food Fact: Turnips are fat free, cholesterol free, low sodium, and an excellent source of vitamin C

This slaw is crunchy and fresh and a wonderful side dish to the heavier winter comfort foods. If you have a mandoline slicer, the prep work of this recipe is a breeze.

METHOD OF PREPARATION

1. In a large bowl, whisk together the orange juice, olive oil, ginger, and salt.

2. Add the Brussels sprout leaves, oranges, turnips, and apple. Toss to coat evenly.

3. Arrange on a platter and sprinkle with the toasted pine nuts.

ROASTED BEET AND JERUSALEM ARTICHOKE CARPACCIO WITH CITRUS SALAD AND MAPLE-GLAZED PISTACHIOS

SERVES 4

GLUTEN FREE, GRAIN FREE, SOY FREE, SUGAR FREE

The colors of this dish are just beautiful. If you can't find golden beets, you can use all red ones. Make sure you wash the sunchokes well, as they tend to have dirt in the crevices, but there is no need to peel them. The earthiness of the beets and artichoke, the freshness of the citrus, the peppery arugula, and the sweet, spicy crunch of the pistachios makes this salad a showstopper. I make a big batch of these pistachios and store them in the freezer. Add them to any salad for a simple elevated touch.

INGREDIENTS

1 cup (140 g) shelled pistachios, roughly chopped

¼ cup (60 ml) maple syrup

1 teaspoon sea salt, divided in half

⅛ teaspoon cayenne pepper

1 large golden beet

1 large red beet

1 tablespoon (15 ml) avocado oil

4 mixed citrus, such as blood orange, pink grapefruit, Sumo tangerine, and Cara Cara orange

1 tablespoon (11 g) Dijon mustard

½ teaspoon freshly ground black pepper

½ cup (120 ml) extra virgin olive oil

⅓ cup (80 g) peeled and thinly sliced Jerusalem artichokes or sunchokes

4 cups (120 g) wild baby arugula

Food Fact: Grapefruits are fat free, saturated fat free, sodium free, cholesterol free, and high in vitamins A and C

METHOD OF PREPARATION

1. Preheat the oven to 400°F (200°C). Line two baking sheets with parchment paper; set aside.

2. In a medium sauté pan over medium-low heat, add the pistachios, maple syrup, ½ teaspoon of the salt, and cayenne. Cook, stirring frequently, until the nuts are toasted and caramelized, about 3 minutes. Spoon onto one of the prepared baking sheets and set aside to cool.

3. Peel the beets and cut into eighths. Arrange in a single layer on the other prepared baking sheet and drizzle with the avocado oil. Transfer to the oven and bake for 30 to 35 minutes or until tender.

4. Section all of the citrus while the beets roast. Remove the peel and pith with a knife. Then cut between the membranes to remove each segment. Squeeze the juice of citrus and reserve.

5. In a medium bowl, whisk together ½ cup (120 ml) of the reserved citrus juice, Dijon mustard, remaining ½ teaspoon salt, and pepper. Slowly drizzle in the olive oil to combine.

6. To assemble, arrange the roasted beets on the bottom of a platter, arrange the sliced Jerusalem artichokes on top, then the segmented citrus, then the arugula, and sprinkle the chopped glazed pistachios on top. Lastly, drizzle with the dressing.

ESCAROLE AND WHITE BEAN SOUP

SERVES 8

GLUTEN FREE, GRAIN FREE, SOY FREE, SUGAR FREE

INGREDIENTS

1 tablespoon (15 ml) olive oil

1 cup (160 g) diced sweet onion

1 cup (120 g) diced celery

6 cups (180 g) roughly chopped escarole
   (about 1 large head)

4 cloves garlic, minced

1 teaspoon dried basil

½ teaspoon dried thyme

½ teaspoon crushed red pepper flakes

6 cups (1440 ml) vegetable broth

One 15-ounce (420 g) can cannellini
   beans, rinsed and drained

CASHEW PARMESAN

1 cup (140 g) raw cashews

¼ cup (10 g) nutritional yeast

½ teaspoon sea salt

½ teaspoon freshly ground black pepper

1 teaspoon garlic powder

Food Fact: Escarole is fat free, good fiber content, contains copper and folate, and a good source of vitamins A, C, and K

Escarole reminds me of my Sicilian side. Whether used in a pasta sauce or in a soup, this bitter green has a special place in my heart. This soup comes together quickly and makes a simple and hearty meal when served with some artisanal bread. The cashew "parmesan" is so delicious. I make a double batch and keep it in the fridge. You'll want to use it on everything.

METHOD OF PREPARATION

1. In a large Dutch oven over medium heat, add the oil. Once hot, add the onion and celery. Sauté, stirring occasionally, for 3 to 5 minutes or until softened and translucent.

2. Add the escarole and garlic and cook for another 3 to 4 minutes or until the escarole has wilted.

3. Add the basil, thyme, red pepper flakes, broth, and beans and bring to a boil. Reduce the heat to low, cover, and simmer for 10 to 12 minutes.

4. While the soup simmers, make the cashew parmesan. In the bowl of a food processor, combine the cashews, nutritional yeast, salt, pepper, and garlic powder. Blend until it resembles grated parmesan cheese, about 1 minute.

5. To serve, ladle the soup into bowls and top with the cashew parmesan.

NAAN FLATBREAD WITH CURRIED CAULIFLOWER, HUMMUS, FRESH HERBS, AND "YOGURT" SAUCE

SERVES 8

GRAIN FREE, SOY FREE, SUGAR FREE

Naan typically contains milk, so making the naan from scratch is a step worth taking. This naan freezes well too, so make an extra batch and keep it in the freezer to make this dish simple to pull together. Aleppo pepper is a specialty, oily red pepper that has a sweet, salty, moderate heat level. You can easily order it online, but if not, you may substitute crushed red pepper flakes.

INGREDIENTS

NAAN

3 cups (360 g) unbleached all-purpose flour

2 teaspoons instant yeast

1 teaspoon kosher salt

1 cup (240 ml) + 2 tablespoons (30 ml) warm water

1 tablespoon (15 ml) maple syrup

2 tablespoons (30 ml) olive oil, divided

CAULIFLOWER

1 large cauliflower (about 2 pounds [910 g]), cored and cut into bite-size florets

1 red onion, halved and thinly sliced

2 tablespoons (30 g) vegan butter, such as Miyoko's, melted

1 teaspoon ground cumin

1 teaspoon ground coriander

1 teaspoon paprika

1 teaspoon freshly ground black pepper

½ teaspoon ground turmeric

½ teaspoon sea salt

2 tablespoons (30 ml) freshly squeezed lemon juice

FOR SERVING

¼ cup (60 g) cashew or almond Greek yogurt

2 tablespoons (30 ml) freshly squeezed lemon juice

1 cup (240 g) good-quality hummus

1 cup (30 g) mixed fresh herbs, such as parsley, cilantro, chives, and mint

1 teaspoon Aleppo pepper

(continued on page 166)

(continued from page 164)

METHOD OF PREPARATION

1. To make the naan, in a large bowl, whisk together the flour, yeast, and kosher salt.

2. In a small bowl, whisk together the warm water and maple syrup. Add the wet ingredients to the dry, and stir with a wooden spoon until combined. Put a little flour on your hands and knead the dough about 20 times or until it forms a nice cohesive ball. The dough will be soft.

3. Place the dough in a lightly oiled bowl, turning it so it is lightly covered in oil. Cover with a dish towel and allow to rise for 30 minutes.

4. Once the dough has risen, place on a lightly floured cutting board. Cut into 8 equal pieces.

5. Heat a large sauté pan or griddle over medium-high heat.

6. While the pan is heating, roll out the dough balls into an oval shape.

7. Add ½ teaspoon of the oil to the pan and add one naan. Cook for 2 minutes per side or until golden brown and puffed.

8. Repeat with the remaining oil and naan breads. This can be done ahead of time and the naan can be frozen for later. Only 4 of the 8 are needed for this recipe.

9. To make the cauliflower, preheat the oven to 450°F (230°C). Line a baking sheet with parchment paper; set aside.

10. In a large bowl, add the cauliflower, onion, melted butter, cumin, coriander, paprika, pepper, turmeric, salt, and lemon juice. Toss to coat.

11. Arrange in a single layer on the prepared baking sheet. Transfer to the oven and roast for 25 to 30 minutes or until tender and golden brown.

12. If your naan is cold, add them to the oven and heat for the last 3 to 5 minutes of the cauliflower cooking time.

13. In a small bowl, whisk together the yogurt and lemon juice.

14. To assemble, divide the hummus among naan, top with the cauliflower, drizzle with a little yogurt sauce, and then sprinkle with the fresh herbs and Aleppo pepper. Serve hot or at room temperature.

CHOCOLATE, GINGER, AND ORANGE CUPCAKES

SERVES 24

GRAIN FREE, SOY FREE

Chocolate and orange are two of my favorite flavors to combine, and with the addition of ginger, these are a little gingerbread, and a lot flavorful. The toppings are up to you, but I personally love all three: candied ginger, orange zest, and cacao nibs. They offer the flavor of the cupcakes in the frosting, pulling the two together.

INGREDIENTS

CUPCAKES

3 cups (360 g) unbleached all-purpose flour

2 cups (400 g) coconut sugar

⅔ cup (80 g) cocoa powder

2 teaspoons baking soda

½ teaspoon kosher salt

1⅔ cups (400 ml) freshly brewed coffee or water

1 cup (240 ml) grapeseed oil

1½ teaspoons vanilla extract

1 tablespoon (15 ml) orange juice

2 tablespoons (16 g) freshly grated ginger

¼ cup (24 g) freshly grated orange zest

¼ cup (40 g) cacao nibs

¼ cup (60 ml) apple cider vinegar

FROSTING

1 cup (240 g) vegan butter, such as Miyoko's, softened

4 cups (480 g) organic powdered sugar

½ cup (60 g) cocoa powder

¼ cup (60 ml) unsweetened almond or cashew milk

1 tablespoon (15 ml) vanilla extract

1 tablespoon (15 ml) orange juice

TOPPINGS (OPTIONAL)

¼ cup (35 g) chopped candied ginger

2 tablespoons (12 g) orange zest

2 tablespoons (16 g) cacao nibs

(continued on page 168)

(continued from page 167)

METHOD OF PREPARATION

1. Preheat the oven to 375°F (190°C). Line two standard muffin tins with paper liners; set aside.

2. To make the cupcakes, in a large bowl, whisk together the flour, coconut sugar, cocoa powder, baking soda, and salt.

3. In another medium bowl, whisk together the coffee, oil, vanilla, orange juice, ginger, and zest.

4. Add the wet ingredients to the dry and stir to combine. Fold in the cacao nibs.

5. Whisk in the vinegar until incorporated.

6. Fill the prepared cups two-thirds full and transfer to the oven. Bake for 15 minutes or until the tops spring back when lightly pressed. Do not overbake and allow to cool completely.

7. To make the frosting, in a large bowl, use a handheld mixer to cream the butter, and then slowly add the powdered sugar and cocoa powder until fully incorporated. Add the milk, vanilla, and orange juice and with the mixer on high speed, beat for 1 minute or until light and fluffy.

8. Once the cupcakes are cooled, frost them.

9. For the toppings, decorate the cupcakes with the candied ginger, orange zest, and/or cacao nibs.

10. Store in an airtight container in the refrigerator for up to 5 days.

NOG

GLUTEN FREE, GRAIN FREE, RAW, SOY FREE, SUGAR FREE

INGREDIENTS

1 cup (140 g) raw cashews, soaked for at least 4 hours, drained, and rinsed

3 cups (720 ml) unsweetened almond milk

6 pitted Medjool dates

1 teaspoon freshly grated nutmeg

½ teaspoon ground cinnamon

1 teaspoon vanilla extract

⅛ teaspoon sea salt

⅓ cup (160 ml) brandy (optional)

Food Fact: Dates are fat free, saturated fat free, sodium free, and a good source of fiber, potassium, and manganese

Eggnog is one of those beverages that you either love or hate; I happen to be on the love spectrum and couldn't wait to create a healthier, plant-based version. I have always felt the original is too thick and creamy, but this one is just right and oh so flavorful! The brandy is optional, but let's be honest, it's one of the main reasons to drink this holiday cheer.

METHOD OF PREPARATION

1. In a high-powered blender, combine the softened cashews, almond milk, dates, nutmeg, cinnamon, vanilla, salt, and brandy (if using). Blend on high speed for 2 to 3 minutes or until completely smooth and creamy.

2. Serve immediately or chill.

PEAR AND DARK CHOCOLATE CHUNK BREAD PUDDING

GRAIN FREE, NUT FREE, SOY FREE

INGREDIENTS

6 cups (600 g) Italian bread in
  1-inch (2.5 cm) cubes

1¼ cups (300 ml) unsweetened almond milk

⅓ cup (80 ml) coconut or date nectar

¼ cup (28 g) ground white chia seeds

1 teaspoon ground cinnamon

½ teaspoon freshly ground nutmeg

1 teaspoon vanilla extract

½ teaspoon sea salt

½ cup (80 g) dairy-free dark chocolate chunks

2 Bartlett pears, ripe but firm, peeled, cored,
  and sliced

Food Fact: Pears are fat free, saturated fat free, sodium free, cholesterol free, an excellent source of dietary fiber, and a good source of vitamin C

Bread pudding is a favorite dessert in my family, one we love to make around the holidays. This one is rich with dark chocolate chunks and sweet pears and sweetened with coconut or date nectar. Don't skip out on allowing the bread to soak up the liquid prior to baking; it really is what makes the pudding light and moist.

METHOD OF PREPARATION

1. Preheat the oven to 350°F (180°C). Grease an 8 x 8-inch (20 x 20 cm) baking dish.

2. Add the cubed bread to the prepared baking dish.

3. In a large bowl, whisk together the milk, coconut or date nectar, chia seeds, cinnamon, nutmeg, vanilla, and salt.

4. Pour the milk mixture over the bread and press down to soak all the bread. Allow to soak for 20 minutes.

5. Sprinkle the chocolate chunks over the top of the bread, pressing them lightly into the pudding.

6. Arrange the pears on top, overlapping to cover the top of the pudding.

7. Transfer to the oven and bake for 25 to 30 minutes or until the pudding is set and golden. Remove from the oven and allow to cool slightly before serving.

NO-BAKE PECAN PIE BITES

GLUTEN FREE, GRAIN FREE, RAW, SOY FREE, SUGAR FREE, UNPROCESSED

INGREDIENTS

1 cup (140 g) organic pecans

8 pitted Medjool dates

1 teaspoon vanilla bean powder

½ teaspoon sea salt

Pecan pie is a Southern winter staple. Growing up with a pecan tree in my backyard made it an easy and perfect addition to the holidays because they are typically harvested from October to December. These no-bake bites are so delicious and way less sinful. They are a wonderful snack or dessert.

METHOD OF PREPARATION

1. Combine all the ingredients in the bowl of a food processor. Process until the mixture is roughly chopped and pulls away from the bowl in a sticky ball.

2. Scooping out teaspoons at a time, squeeze the mixture between your palms and roll into a tight ball.

3. Place in an airtight container and transfer to the refrigerator. Chill for 30 minutes before enjoying.

PEPPERMINT PATTIES

GLUTEN FREE, GRAIN FREE, NUT FREE, RAW, SOY FREE, SUGAR FREE

INGREDIENTS

FILLING

¼ cup (60 g) coconut butter

4 teaspoons (20 ml) water

½ teaspoon peppermint extract

1 tablespoon (15 ml) date nectar

COATING

¼ cup (60 ml) coconut oil

¼ cup (60 ml) date nectar

1 teaspoon cocoa powder

4 teaspoons (20 ml) water

Peppermint patties make an awesome gift or addition to that holiday cookie tray. These could not be easier! You can substitute coconut nectar or maple syrup for the date nectar.

METHOD OF PREPARATION

1. To make the filling, in a small bowl, combine the coconut butter, water, extract, and nectar. Stir well to combine.

2. To make the coating, in another small bowl, whisk together the coconut oil, nectar, cocoa powder, and water. Divide the chocolate mixture in half.

3. In a candy mold, fill the bottom of 8 molds with one-eighth of the chocolate mixture, then one-eighth of the peppermint mixture, then top with the remaining chocolate mixture. Transfer to the freezer and freeze for 30 minutes. If you don't have a candy mold and don't mind your patties looking messy, line a baking tray with parchment paper and add rows of small, 1-inch disks of chocolate until you run out of half the chocolate mixture. Carefully drop the peppermint filling in the center of your disks and press them down to flatten. Then cover in chocolate.

PUMPKIN PIE CRÈME BRÛLÉES

GLUTEN FREE, GRAIN FREE, NUT FREE

INGREDIENTS

Two 12-ounce (340 g) packages silken
tofu, drained

Two 15-ounce (420 g) cans pumpkin puree

1 teaspoon ground cinnamon

½ teaspoon ground ginger

¼ teaspoon ground allspice

¼ teaspoon ground cloves

1½ cups (300 g) coconut sugar

4 teaspoons (10 g) cornstarch

6 tablespoons (72 g) raw organic cane sugar

Food Fact: Pumpkin is fat free,
cholesterol free, sodium free,
a good source of vitamin C, and
an excellent source of vitamin A

Did you ever think you would see a plant-based crème brûlée? These are super simple to make but take a little planning ahead, as they need to be refrigerated overnight. That also makes them easy to serve for a dinner party! All you have to do—and let's be honest, this is the fun part—is torch the top just before you serve them!

METHOD OF PREPARATION

1. Preheat the oven to 325°F (170°C).
Put a kettle of water on to boil.

2. In a high-powered blender, combine the tofu, pumpkin, cinnamon, ginger, allspice, cloves, sugar, and cornstarch. Puree on high until smooth, about 30 seconds.

3. Arrange 6 ramekins or brûlée dishes in a deep casserole pan. Divide the pumpkin mixture among the 6 ramekins.

4. Transfer to the oven and pour boiling water into the casserole dish until it comes about halfway up the sides of the custards.

5. Close the oven door and bake for 40 to 45 minutes or until the edges are slightly browned.

6. Remove from the oven and the water bath and allow to cool completely.

7. Transfer to the refrigerator and chill overnight.

8. When ready to serve, sprinkle each ramekin with 1 tablespoon (12 g) of the sugar and toast with a blowtorch or under your oven's broiler for 2 to 3 minutes (watch carefully!).

9. Serve immediately.

DARK CHOCOLATE
WINTER SQUASH BREAD

SERVES 12

GLUTEN FREE, GRAIN FREE, SOY FREE

INGREDIENTS

½ cup (120 g) unsweetened applesauce

⅓ cup (80 g) cashew or almond Greek yogurt

½ cup (120 ml) coconut oil, melted

½ cup (100 g) coconut sugar

¼ cup (60 ml) aquafaba (chickpea water),
    lightly whipped (see page 54)

¼ cup (60 ml) cashew or almond milk

½ cup (120 g) butternut squash or
    sweet potato puree

2 teaspoons vanilla extract

1⅓ cups (160 g) oat flour

⅔ cup (80 g) unsweetened cocoa powder

1 teaspoon baking soda

1 teaspoon baking powder

½ teaspoon kosher salt

¼ cup (40 g) dairy-free dark chocolate chips

Butternut squash and/or sweet potato makes a perfect vehicle for a tender and decadent bread. Just add dark chocolate and it's a dessert. This quick bread comes together in a snap and will disappear just as fast. You can even make it into muffins, just check for doneness around the 20- to 25-minute mark.

METHOD OF PREPARATION

1. Preheat the oven to 350°F (180°C). Grease an 8½ x 4½ x 2½-inch (21.6 x 11.4 x 6.3 cm) bread pan; set aside.

2. In a large bowl, using a handheld mixer on medium speed, or a stand mixer fitted with the paddle attachment, combine the applesauce, yogurt, and oil and beat until combined.

3. Add the sugar, aquafaba, and cashew or almond milk and mix until light and fluffy, about 2 minutes.

4. Add the butternut squash and vanilla. Beat for 30 seconds to 1 minute to combine.

5. In a medium bowl, whisk together the flour, cocoa powder, baking soda, baking powder, and salt.

6. Add the dry ingredients to the wet and mix until just combined. Do not overmix.

7. Fold in the chocolate chips by hand.

8. Pour the batter into the prepared loaf pan and transfer to the oven.

9. Bake for 45 to 50 minutes or until a toothpick inserted in the center comes out clean.

10. Remove from the oven and let cool in the pan for 1 hour. Flip onto a cutting board and slice.

BAKED APPLES
WITH SALTED CARAMEL SAUCE

SERVES 4

GLUTEN FREE, GRAIN FREE, SOY FREE

INGREDIENTS

1 cup (140 g) walnuts or pecans, chopped

2 tablespoons (30 ml) maple syrup

1 teaspoon ground cinnamon

⅛ teaspoon ground cloves

½ cup (110 g) brown coconut sugar

5 tablespoons (75 g) vegan butter,
　　such as Miyoko's, melted

½ teaspoon sea salt

4 crisp apples, such as Honeycrisp or Modi

¾ cup (180 ml) water

2 teaspoons cornstarch

Baked apples are such a comforting holiday dessert: the smell alone is enough to drive you wild. These have the added benefit of creating their own sauce while baking—a salty sweet sauce, that is.

METHOD OF PREPARATION

1. Preheat the oven to 350°F (180°C).

2. In a medium bowl, mix together the walnuts or pecans, maple syrup, cinnamon, cloves, brown sugar, butter, and salt. Refrigerate while you prepare the apples.

3. Cut the apples in half through the core, then use a scoop to scoop out the core and seeds.

4. Place the apples in a 9 x 13-inch (23 x 33 cm) baking dish, flesh-side up. Scoop the chilled filling into the cavity of each apple.

5. In a small bowl, whisk together the water and cornstarch. Pour around the apples.

6. Cover the baking dish with foil and transfer to the oven. Bake for 20 minutes, remove the foil, and bake for an additional 20 minutes. The filling will be golden and the apples tender.

7. To serve, place the apples in a bowl and spoon the sauce over. Eat while hot!

CASHEW CHEESECAKE WITH DATE WALNUT CRUST

SERVES 8

GLUTEN FREE, GRAIN FREE, SUGAR FREE

This cheesecake is super light and delightful! The crust is chewy and not too sweet, and the filling is lightly flavored with citrus to make it surprisingly refreshing. Plan ahead for this one, as it's best refrigerated overnight.

INGREDIENTS

CRUST

1½ cups (210 g) raw walnuts

¾ cup (135 g) pitted Medjool dates

¼ teaspoon sea salt

FILLING

1 cup (140 g) raw cashews, soaked for at least 4 hours, drained, and rinsed

1 cup (240 ml) coconut cream

8 ounces (225 g) vegan plain cream cheese, such as Kite Hill

1 cup (240 ml) maple syrup

1 tablespoon (8 g) arrowroot powder

1 teaspoon vanilla extract

1 tablespoon (15 ml) coconut oil, melted

1 tablespoon (6 g) orange or lemon zest

2 tablespoons (30 ml) freshly squeezed orange or lemon juice

⅛ teaspoon sea salt

METHOD OF PREPARATION

1. Preheat the oven to 325°F (170°C). Line an 8-inch (20 cm) springform pan with parchment paper; set aside.

2. To make the crust, in the bowl of a food processor, combine the walnuts, dates, and salt. Blend until the mixture is well combined and finely chopped. Press the walnut mixture into the prepared springform pan, allowing the crust to come up a little on the sides. Damp fingers may help this process. Transfer pan to the oven and bake for 15 minutes. Allow to cool while you make the filling.

3. To make the filling, add the soaked and drained cashews to a high-speed blender along with the coconut cream, cream cheese, maple syrup, arrowroot, vanilla, coconut oil, citrus zest, citrus juice, and salt. Blend on high speed until creamy and smooth, 2 to 3 minutes.

4. Pour the filling over the baked and slightly cooled crust. Tap the pan slightly to remove any air bubbles.

5. Transfer back to the oven and bake for 50 minutes to 1 hour, or until the cheesecake is no longer liquid (a little jiggle is okay).

6. Let cool to room temperature for about 30 minutes and then transfer to the refrigerator to cool completely, preferably overnight.

7. To serve, run a knife along the edges of the pan, then carefully open the springform. To slice, use a knife run under hot water and dried.

8. Store any leftovers in the refrigerator, covered.

MINI DRIED FIG AND CHOCOLATE OLIVE OIL CAKES

SERVES 12

GRAIN FREE, NUT FREE, SOY FREE

INGREDIENTS

Coconut oil spray

½ cup (90 g) pitted dates, soaked for
    30 minutes in hot water and drained

¼ cup (30 g) unsweetened cocoa powder

¼ cup (60 ml) hot water

½ cup (60 g) unbleached all-purpose flour

1 tablespoon (12 g) coconut sugar

¼ teaspoon sea salt

¼ teaspoon baking soda

3 tablespoons (45 ml) aquafaba
    (chickpea water), lightly whipped
    (see page 54)

⅓ cup (80 ml) extra virgin olive oil

1 teaspoon vanilla extract

½ teaspoon orange zest

⅓ cup (50 g) chopped dried figs

I love these mini cakes so much. In my opinion, olive oil is not utilized enough in baking. It creates a super tender finished product, with an underlying earthiness in flavor. These come together really quickly and will probably disappear just as fast.

METHOD OF PREPARATION

1. Preheat the oven to 350°F (180°C). Spray a muffin tin with coconut spray; set aside.

2. Add the drained, soaked dates to the bowl of a food processor. Process on high speed until finely chopped.

3. In a small bowl, whisk together the cocoa powder and hot water; set aside.

4. In a large bowl, whisk together the flour, coconut sugar, salt, and baking soda.

5. In a separate medium bowl, whisk together the chopped dates, aquafaba, olive oil, vanilla, and orange zest.

6. Add the wet ingredients to the dry and stir until just combined. Fold in the chopped figs.

7. Fill the prepared muffin cups three-fourths full. Transfer to the oven and bake for 15 minutes or until they spring back when lightly pressed in the center.

8. Allow to cool in the pan for 15 minutes and then transfer to a wire rack. Enjoy warm or all the way cooled. Store any leftovers in an airtight container in the refrigerator.

ABOUT THE AUTHOR

Attending Johnson & Wales University from 2000 to 2004, Melissa Petitto was afforded the opportunities of working for The Governor's House Inn as the bed and breakfast chef and at *Cooking Light* magazine in the test kitchen and graduated with a Bachelor of Science degree in Culinary Nutrition. She received the top honor of *Apprenti Cuisinier*.

After passing her registered dietician's exam, Petitto made the move to New York City to pursue her career goal of becoming a personal chef. With clients, Petitto custom designs menus to fit their lifestyle, health needs, and desires. She shops for the freshest seasonal ingredients at local groceries and farmer's markets to ensure top quality meals.

Melissa has written several specialty cookbooks. Along with this book, she's also written the following titles for the Chartwell Health series: *Adaptogens*, *The CBD Handbook*, *The Celery Juice Book*, and *Superfood Acai Recipes* and others!

Despite her obsession for all things culinary, Ms. Petitto makes time to enjoy other hobbies and passions; attending the ballet, practicing Pilates and yoga, reveling in all things outdoors and spending time with her dog Bella, her husband Brock, and daughter Chloe Skye.

Whether cooking dinner for an individual client or a dinner party for 25, Chef Melissa Petitto, R.D. exudes the passion she feels for nutritious food and its role in a family's life.

INDEX